BETWEEN TWO WORLDS

THE Testimony & THE Testament

David Mittelberg

DE VORA
PUBLISHING
JERUSALEM ◆ NEW YORK

Between Two Worlds:
The Testimony and the Testament
Published by DEVORA PUBLISHING COMPANY

Text Copyright © 2004 by David Mittelberg
Cover and Book Design: David Yaphe
Photo of bag on cover: Yoel Mittelberg

Editor: Chaya Leader

Mittelberg, David.
Between two worlds: the testimony and the testament / by David Mittelberg.
p. cm.
Includes English translation of Testimony, by Israel Jacob Mittelberg.
ISBN 1-930143-88-5 (hardcover : alk. paper)
1. Mittelberg, Israel Jacob, b. 1905 — Imprisonment. 2. Jews — Poland — Warsaw — Biography. 3. Holocaust, Jewish (1939–1945) — Poland — Personal narratives. 4. Concentration camp inmates — Biography. 5. Warsaw (Poland) — Biography. 6. Mittelberg, David. 7. Children of Holocaust survivors — Australia — Melbourne (Vic.) — Biography. 8. Jewish sociologists — Israel — Biography. 9. Israel — Biography. I. Mittelberg, Israel Jacob, b. 1905. Testimony. II. Title.
DS135.P63A152 2004
940.53'18'092 — dc22

2004005171

ISBN: 1-930143-88-5 (HC)
ISBN: 1-932687-08-4 (PB)

Email: sales@devorapublishing.com
Web Site: www.devorapublishing.com

Printed in Israel

Dedication

This book is dedicated to the
blessed memory of my late father
Israel Jacob Mittelberg
and his son Mark
and to all the children and their families
who perished in the Holocaust.

Acknowledgements

This book recounts my father's experiences in the Holocaust and the perspective of his son. It has become a life project in itself and by so doing reflects our indebtedness to so many people without which it would not have reached its current completion.

Sadly as this book was nearing completion, my mother Leah Mittelberg z"l, passed away, in her 86th year on 11 Adar 5764. She was buried next to my father on the following day, 12 Adar, 5764, which is itself the 29th Yahrzeit (anniversary) of my late father's passing. I take comfort in the knowledge that just prior to my mother's passing, she had the opportunity to approve several sections of the final proof, one of the last tasks she undertook diligently and lovingly together with my sister Rachel who was visiting her at the time.

I wish to take this opportunity to acknowledge the tremendous assistance and support of the following people without whose help and constant encouragement this work would not have come to fruition.

In many ways this book has become a family project. Rachel (Mittelberg) Caplan, my only sister and close friend, supported by her husband and my friend Murray, has shared with me all the stages of considering publication the many times we have raised the possibility. From the Yiddish to the English, from the old computer programs to the new, finally, always checking back the final manuscript with the original Yiddish whenever questions arose. Rachel has read the manuscript our late father's and my own, more than once and herself typed the countless corrections that make this manuscript far better than it otherwise would have been.

My daughters Shuli and Esti Mittelberg each in their own way, following their own journey, contributed from their soul to this book and the reader will encounter this for themselves. Sadly my late father did not live to see any of his five grandchildren, for whose health and future he always longed and prayed, but they have built a bridge to his memory and drawn from his legacy nevertheless. I draw strength from their words. Together with their older brother Yoel and cousins Tali and Liora they serve as a third generation testament to the power of memory and its concrete meaning in our lives.

I wish also to thank Mr. Yaacov Peterseil, Publisher of Devora Publishing, who found merit in this book. My thanks also to my editor at Devora Publishing Chaya Leader, and to other proofreaders and copyeditors at Devora for their guidance and assistance. Roberta Bell-Kligler, colleague and friend, found time alongside her responsibilities as Executive Director of Project Oren to meticulously read my manuscript and improve its language for which I am grateful.

Members of Kibbutz Yizreel, the community of my home, have served throughout as a continuing source of support for my work and its translation into everyday life. I would like to record a special thanks to Chana Levine of Kibbutz Yizreel who translated significant sections of my father's manuscript into Hebrew and thereby provided easy access for my children to the life of their grandfather and his heritage.

Finally, this life project would have been inconceivable without the life sustaining support and love of my wife Shoshana. Much has been written in these pages about faith in fellow human beings and the need to bridge time and social differences. The continuing inspiration for the practicality of these values I draw from her love and friendship, without which the story embedded in this book would be hardly of any consequence.

David Mittelberg
Kibbutz Yizreel

Table of Contents

Foreword
Between Two Worlds

Foreword by David Mittelberg

This book contains two parts. Part One: my father's memoirs; Part Two: my life as a one of the second generation of Holocaust survivors. My father wished to share his history with me before my Bar Mitzvah; I wrote this foreword in 1988, with the approach of my son's Bar Mitzvah.

My memory of this manuscript is very distinct. Three years prior to my Bar Mitzvah, in Melbourne, Australia, my father hired a Yiddish teacher, the late Mr. Yehuda Kersh, to teach me Yiddish grammar, Yiddish literature, and so on. Yiddish was my mother tongue; it was the language that I grew up with. I attended a Yiddish kindergarten, however, when I started elementary school, my father decided to place the emphasis on my "Jewish" religious education and sent me to a Talmud Torah, which he deemed mandatory for a Jewish son, rather than the Yiddish Bundist Sunday school which he deemed more appropriate for my sister Rachel to attend. Father was atypically both a lifelong Zionist and also a strong Yiddishist (a supporter of Yiddish culture). However, he did realize that in this way I would miss out on a more serious appreciation of the Yiddish language and culture; therefore, he hired a teacher to pre-

9

pare me for my speech in Yiddish at my Bar Mitzvah.

At that time I knew that my father had also hired Mr. Kersh to edit the memoirs of his experiences in the Holocaust. The experiences themselves were not new to me; they had been told and retold throughout my living memory, every Pesach, indeed at every gathering that my father and his fellow survivors ever held. It did not matter whether it was the formal Warsaw Ghetto commemoration or any other celebration, ceremony, or happy event: each assemblage was an opportunity for conversation on the past including a comparison of the relative suffering of all the participants in the conversation.

I knew that the "tzetlach" (notes) of the memoirs had been recorded in Yiddish immediately after the war, while the memories were fresh and vivid for my father. Having written them, he laid them aside, but with his son's Bar Mitzvah approaching my father decided that perhaps they should be published as a book. Maybe what triggered his decision was a public photo exhibition on the Holocaust which took place in 1956, during which my father was interviewed in the local Jewish and non-Jewish press.

I remember this incident vividly because it was then that I first heard — indirectly — that my father had had another wife and that I had had a brother whom I had never known. My parents did not speak to me about this, apparently wishing to protect me, but the neighbors' children had heard it from their parents and told me. They were incredulous that I had not known. I suspect that from then on I had an intense curiosity about my father's past. Yet let it be clear: my father belonged to those Holocaust survivors who were talkers, and most of the stories which the reader will find in these pages I had heard more than once, more than twice with very little change in the events but perhaps, although of this I am not sure — with a de-emphasis on the violent components. The only thing that was systematically missing in the hundreds of hours of discussion or storytelling in my youth was explicit reference to my father's previous nuclear family.

A few months before my Bar Mitzvah, when my parents were not home, I went to their cupboard and took out the old attaché case which had come with them from Europe; containing, as I knew all their important documents. These included many photos which my father had brought from Europe and which were part of the exhibition in 1956, among them the now very famous photos of the young boy of the Warsaw Ghetto and some other horrible photos depicting executions and Nazi brutality, concentration camps and so on. That night I read the manuscript from beginning to end. The manuscript included a foreword in which my father had written, black on white, that he had lost a wife and a son, and that these words were dedicated to his children just prior to the forthcoming Bar Mitzvah. I was overcome with emotion. Surprisingly, I felt no anger. I decided myself (for whatever that was worth) that the book should be published, and I strengthened my resolve to be a good son for my father in place of the one he had lost.

In 1965 I went to Israel on a year long course on behalf of the Habonim Zionist Youth Movement, to be a youth leader. I met with Dr. Joseph Kermish of Yad Vashem, and we discussed the publication of my father's manuscript, which by then had been received and approved for publication by Yad Vashem in Yiddish. It ultimately transpired that my father decided not to publish the manuscript. He expressed his feelings to me saying, "Who would read my book anyway, there are many such stories in the world. Fewer and fewer people can read Yiddish and those who could are already acquainted with these stories." I suspect that this was not his only reason and that part of it was related to the content of the stories themselves, especially the unspoken parts.

Since that time I have grown up. I have come on Aliyah to

Israel, have married and have three children born in Israel, on Kibbutz Yizreel. In recent years I have begun to ask myself a question: will the memory of the Holocaust continue to the next generation, will it generate a commitment to Jewish survival in my children, as it did in me? Will it have meaning for them or will it be just another ritual in the panorama of memorial rituals that make up the historical Jewish calendar?

Today, in 1988, I am beginning to think about my own son, Yoel Avishai, and his Bar Mitzvah. We are here in Israel at a time of great unrest and uncertainty in many different ways. When Shoshana and I made Aliyah on January 6, 1972 there was much uncertainty in our lives about our future in Israel, on a kibbutz. One thing was certain beyond doubt: my identity and future as a Jew was in Israel; Israel was the most appropriate place in which a modern Jew can and ought to live, where one ought to raise modern committed Jews.

Israel was the answer to the Holocaust philosophically, sociologically and politically, and most of all, it was my personal answer. And yet today what ought to have been the cornerstone of my life in Israel, my Jewishness, turns out to be the focus of social and political controversy. What was supposed to be the *raison d'etre* of being in Israel — namely, being Jewish — is perhaps threatening Israel's future character.

This paradox is in many ways unbearable. It seems intolerable to me that this generation of the Jewish people who witnessed the Holocaust in its most horrendous traumatic form can allow itself or its spiritual and political leadership to endanger both the Jewishness and the sovereign physical future of the Jewish people.

The relevance of the Israeli solution cannot be drawn only from the past; for my children's generation new bases of relevance will have to be generated, and I have no doubt that they will. Yet these cannot be generated in isolation from the past, in disconnection from the past — neither overshadowed nor isolated from it. Not in vain do our sages insist that every generation of Jews should see themselves as if they were at Mt. Sinai, for that is the spiritual source of our humanity and our Peoplehood at one and the same time.

But, I would add that every Jewish person, every Jewish politician, every rabbi, every so-called leader, and certainly all the Children of Israel should see themselves as if they themselves had been miraculously saved from the Holocaust. Why? Not just because of the enormity of the destruction, nor because of its savagery, its brutality, and inhumanity, but because all this savagery, brutality and inhumanity was directed at the Peoplehood of the Jews both in a spiritual and a physical sense. I do not share the somewhat naive view of some of my Sabra friends, in which contemporary Judaism fulfills itself in the everyday life of the Israeli. I reject outright any attempt to cut Israel off from its Jewish past and from its Jewish brothers the world over.

I began by saying that with my Aliyah to Israel, in a sea of personal uncertainty, I was sure of the Jewish solution that Israel offered to my life, and I would say today that if there is anything that is unclear, that cannot be taken for granted, that is being threatened at this very point in time, it is the Jewish character of the Israeli people, and the ability of the Israeli society to continue creatively the tradition of the Jewish people. Will Israel be the place to translate the Jewish heritage successfully into a modern ethos? Will it be a place where all Jews will want to live as Jews, despite the differences between them which are as legitimate, as they are unavoidable? I do not know. However I feel that the commitment to the past has to be a personalized one in order that our collective future will have meaning and potential in our own lives and in the lives of our children. Commitment is a burden; it cannot be taken lightly. Ever since I can remember, it has been explained to me that this is the meaning of being Jewish: assuming additional burdens. Whether at Talmud Torah, the keeping of mitzvot, or the specific social welfare legislation of the Jewish ethos which we preferred to relate to in our semi-secular Zionist youth movements, or again, the universal values which all Jews presumably share, or whether it was in our commitment to *kol Yisrael areivim zeh la zeh* — all the People of Israel are responsible for each other — or whether it was the specific role of the State of Israel with respect to the rest of the Jewish people: all of these are burdens which we have to learn to carry and to pass on to our children.

There are burdens of joy and there are burdens of sadness. A parent who only shares with his children the burdens of joy fails as a parent despite his seemingly good intentions. For responsibility and independence in a child can only be inculcated when he is able to discern, distinguish, and then integrate in his individual life the burdens of joys and the burdens of sadness.

Therefore one continues to live in Israel, shouldering the burdens that life here offers in such multitude; not out of some masochistic, neurotic love of suffering, nor out of any neo-Christian idea that suffering itself has any content - providing purgatory or salvation, there is nothing inherently good in suffering, nothing whatsoever. However, if the suffering has to be, then it must be shared among all of us, for only thus will it be able to guarantee the release from that suffering for all of us.

The story told by my father is one such case of suffering, and it is a case in point for all of us. The events related by my late father are full of minute detail. I do not doubt any of it. They remain as he wrote them in 1945–46 and as they have been re-edited in grammatical Yiddish by the late Mr. Kersh in 1959 and 1960 and translated from the Yiddish by Danielle Charak. My late father read the Yiddish manuscript and authorized its content.

Many years later in Israel, I asked him, "Would you object to me publishing it in English?" He gave me his blessing, saying, "In my view, if it will be published in English, so that people will read it after all, then there may be an important lesson here for the world to learn. For, first of all, they must know and they must not forget. They must know that what I have told happened to real people and it happened to them because they were Jews."

David Mittelberg
Kibbutz Yizreel
Israel

PART I

The Testimony

by

Israel Jacob Mittelberg

𝕱𝓲𝓯𝓽𝓮𝓮𝓷 years have now passed since my release from suffering. Yet still I shudder when I recall those days. Immediately after Liberation I did tell my story to the Jewish Historical Commission, but I did not feel sufficiently relieved. So I

Introduction jotted down my thoughts and memories on scraps of paper. I yearned to divest myself of the weighty burden of remembering and also wished to record some names — some with praise — of those who did well, and of others who did not.

The days after Liberation were a time for bringing back memories, a time when every survivor was a living register of names. The process of recording reunited many families, while confirming for many others that there was no hope of perhaps still finding a loved one alive. On several occasions, I attempted to bring some order to my haphazard notes but, each time, so much surged up in me, that I was forced to give up if I was not to pay the price of suffering once again.

Today it is imperative that I place my experiences on record for the sake of my children. I have established a new home and started a new family with a particularly fine woman: I have two children, a boy and a girl and my son is about to become Bar Mitzvah. I consider it an obligation to acquaint him, on his reaching adulthood, with his father's life and the suffering that being a Jew caused him. This knowledge will strengthen his attachment to our people and our heritage. I hope these simply told words will be useful also to other Jewish children, for they describe the painful path which six million of our people trod. I do not intend to reveal anything new or to make history.

I was in business in Warsaw — knew it, my childhood city, well and knew many people. I was always perceptive of people and knew how to listen to them patiently. Despite the harm that some caused me, I nevertheless believe that man was created in God's image and that he possesses a divine spark. Still today, I love people and enjoy listening to them with empathy, even if I'm not in a position to help them. In the process of recording what I witnessed, I have abridged my notes and left out sections that, at the time, I considered relevant.

I do not wish to alter the style of this manuscript, as the often-sketchy thoughts are an expression of my erratic moods and experiences. My only desire is to add a stone to the memorial of our people. I was destined to live through the horror of Ghetto life and of concentration camps: of Treblinka, Majdanek, Buchenwald, Matthausen, and others.

As the Yiddish poet H. Leivick writes, "I stumbled, rose up and set out again. I met death a thousand times and yet survived."

I owe those who did not survive, whether close to me or less close, to tell the world my story; it is also their story. May their memory continue to live forever.

18

The Ghetto lived with illusions. No one was prepared to believe the horrifying reality and we kept ourselves going on rumors. We greeted each new development with an attitude of "It could have been worse." We found a ray of hope in each

The End of Illusions

German decree — which methodically and assiduously was preparing our total destruction. This was both our good and bad fortune: good, because it helped us endure; bad, because we were deceiving ourselves, thus facilitating the Germans' murderous task.

Up to July 22, 1942, I ran a store at 18 Chlodna Street. Born in Warsaw in 1905, I was married and had one son. From the many important contacts made in my business, I had acquired valuable information, necessary for survival in the Ghetto. Czerniakow, head of the Warsaw Judenrat, was my neighbor and a family friend. It was from him that I learned of the forthcoming akzion (round-up), which would deport only a number and would leave others employed in workshops.

The extermination commando began its activities by shooting people daily. The first to be shot were Bleiman and other well-known businessmen, communal leaders and printers.

On July 22, walking down Grzibowski Street, past the Judenrat headquarters, I noticed the extermination commando in tens of vehicles blocking the entrance to the Judenrat. A great number of the Judenrat were arrested that day.

Two days later, Czerniakow committed suicide, without communicating to the community any information of what lay in store. The reaction among the Judenrat members was one of "each man for himself". Councilor Stolzman, a shrewd businessman, developed a thriving trade with the meager supplies he was handling. He charged heavily for privileges.

During the first stage of the round up, Tebbens, Shulz and others opened workshops, run by Jews. A Jewish engineer working

19

for Tebbens took in only those who owned machines. My sister, the wife of a furrier, found that, in addition to her machine, she also had to contribute a considerable amount of jewelry before being accepted in the workshop. Only those employed, that is, those registered in the workshops, had a right to live. They built bunkers for their families at the workshop premises.

But we soon realized that also the workshops were a ruse to centralize the Jewish population. People were caught like fish during the first blockades on Zamenhof, Gensza, Pawia, and Mila Streets, Muranower Square, Franciskana and Swientojenska Streets. There was nowhere to run. The Jews were taken directly from the workshops to the Umschlagplatz (deportation center) and then to the trains.

The second stage of the round-up consisted of blocking off the street around a particular workshop. I wondered what action to take when the Judenrat closed my store, which was licensed to distribute food on ration cards, on grounds that it was no longer required.

I tried to get employment in one of the workshops. Many offered no work but simply acted as collection centers for Jewish possessions. I got into one, supervised by Karl Heinz Miller. Each workshop had its own living quarters, where it was obligatory for the Jews to live. Tebbens ruled Leszno Street in the small Ghetto. Shulz was master over Nowolipie Street. I worked at 2/20 Walinska Street and also at 27 Zamenhof Street next to 2 Walinska Street. The central headquarters of Miller's workshop were at 9/11 Milna Street. It was here that the blockade took place. The workers were taken out from Walinska Street. Unwittingly, the Germans overlooked 27 Zamenhof Street, which "belonged" to Miller. My wife and I, my child and mother and other inhabitants lay hidden in a bunker. Others were hidden in coal boxes. At the bottom of a wall, a well-concealed trap door could be pulled shut with a rope.

On the following day I emerged from my hiding place believing that the hunt was over. However, I heard shooting and whistling in Milna Street. The Germans had again blocked 9/11 Milna Street to flush out any Jews who had escaped the roundup.

The Jewish police knew me. One of them, Milchman, managed to get me into a police car, a mode of transport I continued to enjoy by special permission of the Jewish police. This luxury gave me the opportunity to observe all the goings-on and warn friends and relatives of any impending akzion. An akzion followed a certain pattern. The commando headquarters were at 17 Ogrodowa Street. Early in the morning, the Jewish police had to line up along Ogrodowa Street, among them the little fellow Leikin, Sherinsky, Stanislav Czaplinski, and Marcel Czaplinski, as well as all the other Jewish police. Each one had charge of a particular section of the Ghetto.

At eight in the morning the Untersturmfuhrer Brandt, whose instructions the local unit awaited in order to begin, used to arrive with his entourage: Oberscharfuhrer Klaster Mayer, Oberscharfuhrer Blescher, Vitasek, and Handske. Their task was to survey the Ghetto each day, map in hand, making notes as to which streets had already been covered, which had not yet, and which were still doubtful.

In order to make it impossible for the Jewish police to alert their own families, Brandt used to first send in the Ukrainian police to the selected spot. Rumors of an impending akzion nevertheless traveled quickly through a variety of channels and emptied the streets of Jews. Only Gentiles, who had broken through the Ghetto fences in order to pillage Jewish homes and possessions could be seen. The Gentiles of Kercelak made a fortune in this way.

The Germans caught some Poles and sent them to 103 Zelazna Street, the administrative center of the Jewish Ghetto, where the stolen goods were taken from them and they were beaten until they promised never to enter the Ghetto again.

It happened once that during one of the blockades on Chlodna Street, they dragged my mother, wife, child, and me out of our shop and we joined the ranks with another ten thousand. I gave a Jewish policeman I knew the key to the shop. My wife prepared the rucksacks. Through a message passed to Czaplinski and Meissler, an interpreter, one of the Oberscharfuhrer approached our ranks, asking, "Wo ist die firma Mittelberg?" ("Where is the Mittelberg store?") he yelled out. We were taken to the K.S.P., *Komendatura Sluzby Porzadkowej,* (Headquarters for the Maintenance of Order); thanks to the delicacies that I still had on my shelves, my family was saved.

After the akzion in the large and small Ghettoes, we were interned in another small Ghetto, which embraced Zamenhof, Gensza, a small section of Nalevkes (numbers 31 49), a section of Franciskaner up to Banifraterska and Swientoyerska Streets up to the Umschlagplatz. There was no end to the killing. The Germans assembled all the Jews employed in the workshops, without exception, on Walinska and Ostrowska Streets, for the purpose of choosing those fit for work. Those selected to go to the left went straight to the Umschlagplatz. Illusions had died; each now knew this was the end.

In September through November 1942, only three thousand Judenrat employees and thirty thousand in workshops were left untouched. The police force was reduced and we now witnessed heartrending scenes of Jewish officers and policemen, in their turn, begging to be spared. Also doctors and engineers, who, up to that time, had enjoyed special privileges, were led to the Umschlagplatz. The little fellow Leikin behaved like a wild animal: he beat anyone who turned to him for mercy. I also scored two blows when I called out to him that he was behaving unscrupulously.

My wife felt life was no longer worth living. I felt lost, but

soon began looking for a way out. I went to try my luck with a sol-
dier in the street and came across the interpreter Meissler with an
Oberscharfuhrer, Kressner. Thousands were clamoring for mercy.
A few hundred people were freed at that time in exchange for gold.

I offered Kressner five kilograms of coffee, sardines, and tea.
He readily accepted. He isolated a group of eleven, among them a
man by the name of Schwalbe, and led us to 10 Novolipki Street.
We walked in fear of being seen by Brandt. A week later we were
taken back to the small Ghetto. By then it was perfectly clear to us
that no workshops, assurances, or fitness for work would guarantee our lives. Our intended end was obvious.

A new chapter of suffering, hopes, dreams, and tragedies began
— that of life in the bunkers. An obsession overcame the remnants
of the population: only in bunkers was it now possible to survive.

The underground movement began to intensify its activities.
To finance their operations, they demanded money from the richer
Jews and also from the policemen who extorted money from possible victims. The policemen who refused to pay up were shot
without ceremony. The underground movement also made
attempts on the lives of several particularly hated Ghetto rulers.

Chzezinski, a cruel and objectionable human being, in charge
of the Umschlagplatz, had accumulated a lot of money. From him
the underground demanded a large sum. As he simply shrugged
off their demands, he was taken from home and shot in an attic.
Leikin also came to a bad end. As he was leaving 4 Gensza Street
one evening with his deputy, Czaplinski, two bullets pierced his
skull and he fell down dead. Czaplinski, a reasonably decent sort
of fellow, was lightly wounded.

Another policeman, Firstenberg, was also condemned to death
by the underground and his sentence was duly carried out.
Following these executions, the German authorities no longer
relied on the Judenrat for assistance and took it upon themselves

to keep order without consulting any Jewish groups. This step convinced everybody, even the members of the Judenrat, that we could not delude ourselves any further.

When speaking of life in the bunkers, one must begin by expressing admiration for the ingenuity and inventiveness that human beings exhibit. Secondly, one must examine a range of social and moral issues, which are relevant not only to psychologists and philosophers, but also to us simple folk, the rank and file of society.

Life in the Bunkers

In the bunkers, we were faced with, and had to find practical solutions to the issues of the individual versus the collective, of responsibility and self-sacrifice, of the right to make decisions about another's life for the "good" of the group and also the issue, forever fresh, of akeidas Yitzchak (the Sacrifice of Isaac). Generations of thinkers, philosophers and writers have grappled with these issues but none were placed in the situation we were in: without adequate preparation, we were forced to make hasty decisions on these concerns. It was asking too much of us and many tragedies resulted.

The bunkers were built with much ingenuity. A cellar measuring ten meters was reduced to two. Thirty to forty people could hide in that small area. Builders, locksmiths, plumbers, and electricians were required for the reconstruction. Power was drawn from the tramway lines. We prepared provisions, mostly dry biscuits and soup cubes.

The first bunker I organized was in a cellar at 30 Zamenhof and 22 Gensza Streets. It consisted of three rooms in a cellar, which was cut off from another and was concealed by boxes. We built a wall, dried it out with small coke ovens, and dirtied it to give it an aged appearance. One entered the bunker through a brick trap in the wall, which could be opened from inside the cellar. We also made another bunker on the sixth floor, an attic, which could be reached through the toilet of a fifth floor apartment occupied by Leon Shimkewicz. We removed the ceiling of the toilet and inserted a sheet of thick cardboard with a sand finish into which we fitted a light bulb. We painted it and attached a rope and ladder to it. From the outside one could not suspect this hiding place. Shimkewicz, Aaron Stock, and I decided to establish this additional hiding place due to the fact that too many people knew about the bunker in the cellar.

The job had to be executed with care and precision. We smuggled bricks and ten buckets of cement from the yard of the Judenrat, located across the street from us. We set up a toilet in the hiding place and two observation points, one onto Zamenhof, the other on Gensza, Franciskana, and Nalewkes Streets. We saw the Ukrainians, Latvians, and SS hiding in the entrances to the houses, armed from head to toe.

When Piszyc, Leikin's deputy, heard that we were building a bunker, he advised us of a forthcoming akzion and begged us to take in not him, but his wife, his child, his sister, sister-in-law, and brother-in-law, Dr. Zadrewicz.

On the eve of Pesach 1943 we were given honey, sugar, and matzos at around midday. We still believed we would celebrate the Seder, although we knew from experience that on every Jewish festival the Germans invented some new cause for "rejoicing."

The Last Round-Up (Akzion) At ten at night the rumor spread that the Ghetto would be surrounded during the night. At midnight we heard the sighs and sobs of those who were packing their belongings to go into hiding in the bunkers (if they had any). Each fought for a better position. We lay in wait. At four in the morning, we heard cars arriving. The commando examined the Ghetto and at seven o'clock it all began.

Units of soldiers arrived and stopped at the little garden adjoining the Judenrat headquarters; minutes later we heard shooting. One of the policemen brought us a few guns and several hundred bullets. We decided to put up a resistance. Shimkewicz had, on the evening of April 19th, received some ammunition from the Poles. We were in touch with the illegal underground. Every evening, Pyszyc and his deputy, Kac, brought us news of the outside world. Kac held out no hope that anyone would survive. "You will die upstairs and I downstairs," he said. After several days Pyszyc and Kac came no more. They were shot with the rest of the Judenrat and the Jewish policemen in the yard of the Judenrat headquarters.

Unfortunately, a terrible accident occurred. The central Ghetto pharmacy situated in the building where we were hiding contained flammable materials. The gas pipes were cut and the escaping gas poisoned many hiding in the bunkers. The trap resting on iron rails proved too heavy to be opened quickly. We found Stock's charred body by the open trap. He must have managed to open it finally, but only three or four people had had time to escape. The others were simply too weak to break through the fire. Burning debris was flying through the air: the smoke was suffocating. To run out into the street meant certain death.

A friend of mine, Igelberg, a mechanic and locksmith in the Jewish police, suggested we go to a bunker in 18 Gensza Street. My wife and child, my sister, Stock's wife, and child and Igelberg with his wife and child made our way up the partially burnt staircase of the Gensza building. Igelberg knocked at the door and told them that he was alone. When they opened the door we all pushed our way in. The bunker belonged to Rabbi Meir, the caretaker of the house. We were concerned for Igelberg's three-month-old baby.

Some worried that there was not enough oxygen for the numbers in the bunker.

After several hours we began examining our common fate. There were bunks in the hiding place awaiting some occupants who had not made it to the bunker in time. We found ourselves in a terrible situation, in constant fear for our young children's lives, as well as for our own. Yet we could not give in, for, if the men showed weakness, everything was lost. We were, however, growing weaker and the provisions were diminishing, particularly for those who had been running from one bunker to another. Those with supplies had no wish to share them and this caused squabbling. I felt that the adults would in some way make it through but the children had to be fed. We asked Rabbi Meir for some food for the child. He refused. He relented only when I offered him some brandy and cigarettes.

The problem with the children was very serious in the bunkers particularly for those whose fathers were no longer with them. And there were Isaac's two little girls who had lost both parents. Other fathers did not wish to take on that burden and there were some tense moments; one involved my friend Igelberg, who experienced a tragedy.

Every whisper, every noise was a risk for those in the building, as the Germans were constantly searching for survivors. The angry bunker occupants feared that the cries of the three-month-old baby would betray them all. Some considered that a baby should not jeopardize the safety of the majority. But how can one ask a mother to terminate the life of her recently born child? One hundred and sixty people confronted that difficult question which has never been resolved by the greatest thinkers and philosophers. We went out of our minds. Some suggested the child should be poisoned or suffocated. The mother wanted to die with her child.

Seeing the tragic consequences of the situation it was suggested to leave the child's life to fate: the child should be dressed in its best clothes and we should attach a note to it saying it is a Polish child and asking for the child to be sent to Gentile friends of the Igelbergs. The child was put to sleep with a little alcohol, and with the parents' agreement the child was taken away. Even this caused argument. One camp did not trust the other. Finally it was decided that the father would go (not the mother because of her tears), a young man from the "opposing camp", and I.

We crawled through openings in the walls up to 32 Zamenhof Street and sped back. But the child's parents were unable to endure this tragedy and the same night, against our wishes, left the bunker. We were later told that their bodies were seen on Milna Street; they had both been shot.

Once, in the middle of the night, we heard knocking underground. We thought the Germans had tracked us down. All night the knocking continued and when it was already quite close, we asked in Yiddish, "Who is it?" A few voices begged us to let them in. In the bunker, some felt that no one should be allowed in; there was neither enough food, nor space, nor anything else.

I was of the opinion that we must help them as they had arms, supplies, and matches (according to what they were saying). In any case, I argued, they would break in. We agreed to let them in but told them to return during the night when there were less Germans around, since Ghetto-fighters had been organizing attacks on Nazis under cover of night.

To our disappointment, the new arrivals had brought nothing with them other than two revolvers. The situation was deteriorating, particularly for the children. The two little orphans were dying of hunger. Mrs. Warszawska and her little boy said nothing but kept close to us. My wife was a fine, caring woman. Whatever food she received she shared with them. My son was quite resilient despite his delicate constitution. He wanted nothing to eat but clung to me, unwilling to let go of me for a moment.

It was vital that we procure food for ourselves. We knew that there was some in the neighboring bunkers. The Germans had uncovered those bunkers, but they and the Ukrainians used to take only gold and valuables. The food, sometimes soaked in water, sometimes burnt, they would leave behind. However, we had no option but to try to get to it.

We crawled through to 34 Zamenhof Street and ran across the street. It was midnight. We could not light any matches and fell into a cellar where the stairs had been burnt out. We were badly bruised but continued on our mission. I knew the bunker well; it was the one I had built with Stock. I knew there were many provisions. I knew exactly where the entrance was.

While knocking down the bricks of the bunker we heard shooting from the direction of our cellar. I decided we should stop and wait. For three hours we lay and waited while the shooting continued. Finally, we made our way in. The smell of the corpses did not deter us. We rushed to taste the matzos, schmaltz, and eggs we had prepared for Pesach. We took the supplies, some of which were now spoiled. The bunker was under water and we were standing in it. Suddenly, we heard human voices. Two Jews had survived a raid by the Germans in a neighboring bunker as they stood on guard at another entrance. They had managed to hide while the others were being led away, denounced by a fellow Jew. And now they felt guilty, having heard the cries of their loved ones, as they lay in hiding. We decided to take them back with us.

There was much rejoicing when we returned. Our families thought we had fallen into German hands. We also thought we were dead many times during this dangerous expedition. We feared falling into the hands of the Germans for two reasons. They tortured those they captured to extract from them information on the location of bunkers. Some could not endure the pain and some believed naively, that, if they offered them the information, the Germans would grant them their lives. This, and the shortage of food explained the difficulties strangers had in being accepted into a bunker.

I had to undertake to look after the two men I had brought back. One other elderly, respectable occupant of the bunker helped me to convince the others to allow the two men to stay with us. We did not sleep, neither that night nor the next few. We still held onto hope, despite our wretched plight. We wanted to believe that the uprising was an indication of Hitler's demise.

Meanwhile our supplies were running out. We were living close to the Judenrat's vegetable stores. That night we walked through the blazing, brightly lit streets in flames. We raided the storeroom and brought back carrots, beetroots and potatoes. We were all overjoyed but the supplies also caused fights. Everyone wanted to run and get some. This we could not permit for fear that the weak or old would be caught and forced to denounce the location of the bunker. The supplies were therefore equally divided and it was decided that only the younger, stronger, and more agile occupants should go out. We agreed to die rather than divulge the whereabouts of a bunker. We had some ammunition and agreed to defend ourselves.

We ate the vegetables raw. We cooked the potatoes on an improvised stove of bricks placed on the gas pipes. Each family took turns, cooking every third day. One day we noticed that the children were fainting. It turned out that too much gas was escaping from the pipes, a mishap which put an end to our cooking arrangements. When the greens ran out we ate the potatoes raw. Again, five of us, armed with pistols, set out in search of food.

It was ten o'clock in the evening and pitch black. We followed the same route as previously but suddenly fell into a ditch where the storeroom had been. The Germans had bombed it, having found human imprints around it. We were badly bruised and picked ourselves up with difficulty. Yet we dragged ourselves together and set about rummaging for food. To our delight, we found a very special delicacy, sauerkraut — all that was left. Others had beaten us to raiding the storeroom. We now had to get ourselves out of the ditch. We stacked boxes and other items on which to climb out when we heard the noise of a motorcycle of a German patrol. Luckily, they did not hear us, and we got back to the bunker safely.

All were happy to see us. But the situation was not improving. As well as the shortage of food, the heat in the bunker was intolerable. We forbade smoking in order not to use up any oxygen. People were so desperate that some preferred to leave and die from a German soldier's bullet. But we could not let them go for fear they would give out information about us under torture.

One morning we heard some knocking. The voice of a woman called my name and begged to be allowed in with her children. It was Mrs. Windman, with two children, her mother, and the brothers Kopchuk. It was clear to me we had no choice but to let them in, yet the other occupants were staunchly opposed. The arguments continued all day; we almost came to blows. Those most adamantly opposed to accepting outsiders were those who still had some provisions. Softly, we, who were in agreement to let them in, instructed them when to come back and to use the entrance on Zamenhof Street.

We waited in vain. They never came. If, as we feared, the Germans had caught them, we were also lost. We learned later, that, indeed they had been picked up by the Germans and taken to the Umschlagplatz but they had not given us away. The following evening at 10 P.M. we heard knocking. We were standing close to the wet walls in a bid to cool off a little. Our nerves were taut, the knocking seemed ominous, the children were crying, the adults were packing their belongings. Even in moments like these, people worried about the few things they owned.

Yet, to our astonishment, a group of Jews appeared in the opening, a group of courageous people who had made their way through ruins and dug passages to the Aryan side to enable them to escape. They crawled through holes with great agility, finding their way literally from under the ruins. They were in the same position as we, without means of livelihood, without room for the hundreds of survivors of other burnt-out bunkers, seeking a place of refuge.

Among them I saw many who had worked in the vegetable storeroom. Rabbi Meir whispered to one who knew my brother-in-law, Ackereisen, that I still had some alcohol on me. He did this to detract the attention from himself and the provisions he still had, which he wanted to share with no one, not even with the young children. He had taken over a section of the cellar and there closed himself off with his provisions. I bartered with one of the newcomers, agreeing to exchange some of my alcohol for dry biscuits for my son. I gave him the alcohol but never received the biscuits.

The new arrivals asked us to take in another thirty survivors. The arguments broke out again. We need not have bothered; the Germans had their own plan for them. On their way back to their bunker their tragic fate already awaited them. Their bunker was already under observation and the Germans and Ukrainians led them to the Umschlagsplatz. I only remember the baker Hartman and his sons in that group. Their end demoralized us further. They were a heroic gang and their bunker had many exits to facilitate an escape.

We were all very worried. Only Reb Meir believed he would survive and refused to share any of his supplies. When his brother-in-law was in great need of some alcohol, he sent him to me and in return begrudged me two small crackers.

It all happened at eight the next morning. We heard shooting and whistling from both sides; Germans and Ukrainians broke in, yelling, "Hands up!" They swore at us and demanded money and gold, under threat of shooting us on the spot. We each gave what we had and they stuffed it into their pockets. One officer told us we were being transported to work. We accepted that lie also and squeezed out of the cellar.

The Germans had come from the same opening as our guests of two days earlier; quite clearly they had denounced us. Some young ones hid as we were marching out. Those with families stayed close to them amid sobs and cries. We felt like animals being led out of cages. Outside, we caught sight of the two young men who had denounced us — one was eighteen, the other in his early twenties. They tried to deceive us, further assisting the Germans in their treacherous work. They told us lies: that we were being taken for work, that all the bunkers had been discovered, that we were the last. That too was a lie. The same Nazi who had assured us a few minutes earlier that we were being transported to work, now informed us that only those who revealed the whereabouts of other bunkers would be taken to work. The informers were often put to death before their victims.

A selection took place. About one hundred and sixty of us stood for an hour in the yard. Those prepared to talk were told to move to the right. Out of our ranks, no one volunteered except for a couple by the name of Shuster — he had served as a Jewish policeman. We turned away from them in contempt.

We were made to stand in rows and, accompanied by blows and curses, we were led through Gensza to Nalevki and Franciskana, Streets. At 24 Gensza Street, bordering with 37 Franciskana Street there was a fenced-off, desolate field where we were subjected to a full examination and search. We were taken in, a few at a time, while the others waited at the corner of Gensza and Nalevki Streets, guarded by Ukrainians and Latvians. The SS carried out the inspection, led by a young SS officer who forced each and every man and woman to strip naked while yelling at us and beating us.

The inspection was a horrifying ordeal. All parts of our bodies were searched, every ring torn off our fingers while the SS officers laughed with derision at us, their victims.

Some in the group, nevertheless, still clung to the hope that we were, in truth, being transported to work. These optimists prepared supplies of sweets, taken, in fact, from the community's stores — sweets which were more precious than the juiciest orange. Some were of the opinion that we should have listened to the Jewish police who, during the first days of the uprising, had advised us to volunteer for work in Poniatov or Trawnike. Most of us, however, refused contemptuously to accept such deception. It was clear to all that there was one road, via the Umschlagsplatz, to Treblinka. Therefore, few were duped and, whoever was able, put up some resistance.

The brush workers at 28-30-32 Swientaiedka Street put up the most heroic and prolonged resistance. They killed the greatest number of Germans. The German attack, led by a general together with high-ranking military officials, was determined to capture the "fortress."

While waiting in line to be checked out we met many survivors. Each inquired after the other's family and friends. We still hoped that a number of Jews were left hiding in the bunkers but names of uncovered hiding places and their occupants kept being mentioned. The Germans used not only informers but also the latest bugging devices and airplanes. Wherever they suspected that humans were hiding, they threw grenades and hand bombs.

Thousands died buried under the ruins.

After the check-out we were lined up. I noticed two of the group disappear at 27 Nalewki Street, in a deserted house, while the guards had their backs turned. Many of us thought to do the same, yet there was not much point, since Ukrainians and Latvians surrounded the Ghetto.

There were corpses everywhere. Some were still dressed in their best clothes. One wore one's best clothes for that final journey. But the majority were naked, stripped by the Ukrainians who sold the clothes to the Poles at the gates of the Ghetto.

The march began. The Ukrainians relentlessly forced us to run on the double. We could hardly walk nor move; we were weary, hungry, and thirsty after so much suffering. And the heat was intolerable. The children were particularly weak and had to be carried, which prompted the thugs to force us to move even faster. Whoever fell was shot on the spot. We were told this was no time for a stroll. Whoever could not walk fast would remain lying in the streets. We saw Pinkert, the funeral director, accompanied by two others, ride into their home at 40 Zamenhof Street. We hardly managed to ask him what was going on. His answer was curt; "You are the last of the last." Pinkert was very diligent but he could not keep up with taking all the dead to the cemetery in his one and only cart.

We walked the whole length of the Nalevkes. Every meter was covered with mutilated, bloodied bodies. We reached Pakarna Street, near the Muranover square; there were bodies strewn everywhere, some decomposing. Ruins surrounded us; there was death and blood everywhere. Only the fire, the glowing, flying chunks of metal, and the crumbling walls offered a sign of life. Such was the death march to the death square.

Still today, a chill runs down my spine when I hear what seems an innocent enough word: Umschlagplatz. My most tragic memories are connected with this word, which in Yiddish simply means "square for transfer." Maybe the word was

The Umschlagplatz suitably chosen, for here people were indeed transformed: the concept of humanity was destroyed. On one side were the torturers, wild animals; helpless, unfortunate, weak creatures were on the other side.

Here, in the Umschlagplatz, life came to an end. However miserable life had been in the Ghetto, it was familiar and one still felt in control. Here, the slow, gradual death began, not of the individual but of Klal Yisrael. Some found death on the spot; others began on the painful journey, the theme of which was death. Whoever had a shorter journey suffered less than those who survived all the tortures and pain and died at the time of the Liberation or close to it.

The Ukrainians were in charge of the Umschlagplatz, since the Germans feared infection of contagious diseases. The building was large and could accommodate great numbers of people. The spot was notorious already at an earlier stage, when the transports had passed that way, supposedly to be taken to work. It had, at one stage, been possible to buy off the guards and be freed or to use one's influence to get someone out. But now there was nothing left to do; all were reduced to the same wretched state.

Everyone raced off to take up a position in the building, each with his own calculations. Some reckoned the upper floors would be cleared first into the trains; others said the lower floors. I went up to the fifth floor with my wife, son, and my eldest sister. The Ukrainians ordered us to sit on the floor and forbade us to take even as much as a drink of water. Even those naive enough to believe that we were being sent to work, were losing hope. We sat in total silence for several hours. We feared the Ukrainians more than the Germans and the former indeed showed what they were capable of.

When one of them came in and asked for money, a Jew from Lodz offered him five hundred zloti, upon which the Ukrainian demanded five thousand under threat of shooting him. Kac didn't know what to do. If he acceded to his request, the guard would demand more, and if he didn't.... All the others signaled him not to give in, so the routine would not be repeated with them. The Ukrainians ordered the man to undress and all others to dance around him. Old people, unaccustomed to dancing, were forced to jump about. Other Ukrainians requisitioned our boots, yet I managed to keep mine, telling them that the Germans had taken my money when searching us.

The second shift of guards invented a new game. They chose two young men and ordered them to fight. Of course they fought lightly, both out of humanitarian consideration and out of sheer weakness. Not satisfied, one of the Ukrainians demonstrated how it should be done. Blood was streaming down their bodies. They both had to fight until they collapsed. The young children trembled as they witnessed all this. My friend Zlotikamien sat across from me. We lived through a few camps together and he also survived. Next to him was Pastak, an observant Jew, with a black beard, a Modzicer Hasid of good standing. His face was dark, looking at the painful sights. He had a suspicion that the scoundrels would start picking on him so he whispered to his neighbor that he had some jewelry sewn into his coat. The Ukrainian turned around, caught sight of him and ordered him up. He aimed his rifle at him. At first we thought he simply wanted to frighten him but soon we heard the shot splattering his brains against the wall. Two Ukrainians threw the body out of the window.

Another Ukrainian called a young woman from one end of the room and a young man from the other and forced them to have intercourse. There was no limit to the horror, wildness and inventiveness of the torture to which they subjected us. We lost every glimmer of hope and prayed for a speedy death.

My darling, modest wife begged me that we should commit suicide rather than witness such pain and shame. She said it was God's will that Jews were doomed to die. I tried to convince her that man must hold on to life as long as he lives. That much I had learned from life. Those who had given in had sealed their fate.

My saintly son, hardly twelve years old, always one to raise everyone's spirits, was taking in the scene with his beautiful blue eyes. He had been reading the newspapers and had wanted to convince us all along that the time of liberation was approaching. He had believed that the present situation could not last and that victory must come. Here on the Umschlagplatz, he sat resigned and silent. He understood the end had come and he did not want to cause us hurt. I wanted to console him but his answer was, "Daddy, everything is over. We are standing on the threshold of destruction." We wept and waited for our destiny.

Nevertheless, I tried to make contact with the Ukrainian guards, fully aware that even were we to be released from the Umschlagplatz, we had nowhere to go. Release from captivity hardly ensured salvation. Yet I had to try. Nothing came of these negotiations. We sat at the Umschlagplatz for three days. My little boy did not let go of my hand. Our nerves were so strained that when we were driven into the trains to our death we considered it some kind of deliverance. Many had developed an approach of equanimity towards life and death. Others found the courage to endure any painful ordeal in the faintest flicker of hope of survival.

I cannot judge which was worse: the road to Treblinka or being in that slaughterhouse of three million. The days and nights of wailing and slaughter, beatings and cursing, blood and death, all add up to a nightmare beyond description, beyond imagination.

On The Road To Treblinka At nine in the morning we were hustled to the trains, starting from the upper floors. The noise, sobs, cries filled the air. The whole exercise was carried out with speed. Families clung to one another in order not to lose one another during these last hours of life. My wife on one side, my son and sister on the other, we climbed down the stairs where armed SS guards were ready to shoot in case of an attempted escape. One hundred and twenty people were squeezed into each wagon; later, another thirty were pushed in. We stood on top of each other.

I passed Mrs. Kirszenbaum, a neighbor, who told me that our landlord, Joseph Shoenberg, had died under the ruins of one of the workshops. Mrs. Kirszenbaum herself later disappeared. Her husband was shot by the Ukrainians while attempting to escape. She jumped with him. Her brothers-in-law never knew whether she had survived or not.

We had not a drop of water. The heat and lack of space were suffocating. People fainted. The children were particularly badly off. Their mothers gave them urine to drink to wet their dried-out lips. People simply were dying off. The dead remained standing buttressed by the living. We were so desperate — we knew that the Ukrainians and Latvians perched on the roof of the train, would shoot at any protruding head; still, some attempted to jump.

Each wagon had a window, forty by thirty centimeters in size, and we could lift a person up to the window to push him out. Hardly anyone managed to survive, since the guards opened fire immediately and incessantly. Frequently, the corpse fell back into the wagon. If they could reach, the guards even fired into the wagons. Each time they hit someone they broke out in a murderous laughter; all the while they drank alcohol.

Those parents not contemplating jumping organized some space for their children near the locked doors where, through a chink, they could inhale some fresh air. We stood around the children to save them from being squashed. The instinct to live is strong. It inspired thoughts and dreams of the Nazis' imminent defeat, and therefore, renewed our own desire to live.

But how to remain alive, that one did not know. Of those who jumped, very few survived. Those who escaped the bullets only then began their torturous journey. We knew our Polish neighbors too well to expect more than contempt for our plight. We knew they would hand us over to the Germans with glee, if they did not finish us off first.

Goldberg, a Jew from Warsaw, threw his two-year-old out of the window on the off-chance that it might live. He kept his older girl of ten with him. His wife and daughter died in Treblinka and he, who had the good fortune to come out of Treblinka and worked in Skarszysk at some lighter work, also died of hunger. What happened to the two-year-old, no one knows. We noticed that we were traveling in the direction of Szedlec Malkin. Now there was no doubt in anyone's mind that we were being led to the Treblinka ovens.

My heart ached at the fate of my darling wife and son. In better days, everyone had envied me my wife and son. Life had been a short dream. My wife, Roma, begged me to jump; perhaps it would be my good fortune to survive. She didn't want my decision to be dependent on her. I wanted her to be the first to jump, then our boy, and only then me. She did not agree, pointing out that the window was too small for her to get through with ease and that the shooting did not let up. I nevertheless decided to remain with them, come what may.

The train was approaching Treblinka. The wagons were dripping with blood. The occupants were stepping over bodies, both dead and alive. Human beings were now like animals. We quenched our thirst with urine. The air was filled with cries and wailing, but without an echo. The Gentiles at work in the passing fields heard and saw and ignored it all. Totally abandoned and helpless, we were being led to the slaughter.

Treblinka offered us a warm welcome: as we stepped off from the trains, we were greeted by the SS and their dogs with yells and screams, which completely bewildered us. That was precisely the intention of these civilized animals. No

In Treblinka
guns were required for our exhausted bodies. So as to avoid disorder, *ordnung muss doch sein.* Order must prevail. Avoiding disorder was behind every German command. It was all done with such speed that no one managed to grasp how a transport of ten thousand people could disappear through the gas chambers. The Germans kept strong men as well as good-looking women to serve their own purposes.

The Jewish commando consisted mainly of underworld types, carriers and coach drivers whom I had known in earlier days. I met them now at the entrance gates of the camp. They were led by an engineer, Galewski from Lodz. In the Warsaw Ghetto he had been in charge of the cosmetics workshop at 70 Leszno Street. I asked him for some advice. He did not turn to look at me, despite my repeated efforts and the fact that he knew me well. My friend Reisman, who took part in the uprising in Treblinka, told me afterwards that Galewski was a decent human being, but was unable to help much and in the conditions that prevailed, one hardened and lost all human feeling.

The Jewish commando was divided into brigades, one brigade

cleared the trains of any remaining belongings: people simply left things behind out of apathy and resignation. Another brigade, the corpse-brigade, dragged the dead out of the wagons. A third brigade was in charge of collecting all valuables, including money, for the Germans. They surrounded us and yelled at us to hand over all gold, jewelry and watches before the Germans searched us. They walked around with a large blanket and everyone threw in whatever precious items they still possessed. There were other brigades involved in a variety of activities in connection with the death chambers, but I didn't come in contact with them. The Jewish commando was present at the arrival point and contributed to the yelling and the general pandemonium.

The SS were yelling orders that men and women separate. I said farewell to my wife. She moved to the women's ranks with tears in her eyes. Despite the suffering we had shared, we were not destined to remain together up to the end. She said farewell to me with the words, "Live, Richard." She had, through her grief, noticed that the Germans were singling out some men and intuitively had recognized that they were to live. So she sent me there and entrusted me with our son. The orders were that the children were to go with the women, yet she thought that maybe she could smuggle him through with me. She returned to me several minutes later with a bag containing some underwear, a little food, and jewelry. Under cover of the general commotion she thought she would go unnoticed. But a German caught sight of her, took away the bag and struck our son with a whip back to the group of women. My little boy, who had already said upon arriving in Treblinka, "Daddy, it's all over," moved away, resigned to his fate. I tried to plead, but in vain. I wanted to run towards him. The SS stopped me. I did not even have the joy to take my son in my arms a last time and bid him farewell.

Such were my last moments with my loved ones on the

slaughter field. Shortly afterwards, they went through the gate, the border between life and death. This was the most difficult moment in my life. Neither the earlier suffering nor the later ordeals broke me as much as that moment when I was granted life.

Despite warnings from the brigade in charge of removing all valuables not to hide anything, I did keep a few precious belongings, fully aware that if I were discovered during the search I could pay with my life. No Jew takes his own life, but for me, life had lost all meaning, and it may be that that very equanimity blunted me for the ensuing trials and tribulations that still faced me.

The Jewish commando brought us some buckets with water as if we were horses. Indeed, that is all we now were, horses; the coach drivers with their whips felt responsible that the horses be given water. We were then ordered to sit down. We were guarded by a group of Ukrainian guards on a hill. There was dead silence. Only an hour had passed and no one remained of the ten thousand who had arrived on our transport train. Only we five hundred and seven sat there, awaiting our fate.

A young and pretty Jewish girl went by in search of people she knew. She told us no one had survived. The whole procedure lasts only minutes, she reported. As they pass through the gate they are forced to undress quickly. The clothes brigade removes the clothes for sorting according to the value of the fabric. All victims are then driven into another room where one must throw off everything one is carrying and one remains stark naked. There is a path through an open gate to the showers, the gas chambers, cynically named by the Germans Himmelstrasse, "the path to Heaven." There the Germans do not keep count any more; they simply pack the people in. The Germans commit such tortures at that stage that the horrible death is considered deliverance. Specially trained dogs held by the Germans on "the path to Heaven" tear at the passing victims, at their sexual organs.

After the liberation, I was in Treblinka with my friends, survivors of the Treblinka uprising. We were accompanying a Commission of Inquiry under the auspices of the Jewish Historical Commission led by Captain Kermish and the writer Rachel Auerbach. My friends said that when the doors of the gas chamber were opened, the people were blue and so pressed together as to be unrecognizable. Mounds of corpses were then burned. The ash of the bones still lay on the fields. I picked up a bone, maybe that of one of my dear ones.

We five hundred and seven sat sadly listening to the distant noises; then, all fell silent. I had been in Treblinka only five to six hours, yet it seemed like an eternity. There were some who so desired to live that they did not feel the last breath and heartbeat of the ten thousand who had, until an hour ago, been with us. They did not feel that we were now on the most tragic cemetery of all times. They laughed and rejoiced. The Treblinka Jewish commando envied us, since they knew that once their job was done, they would also end up in the gas chambers.

We were the lucky ones; how tragic the word "lucky" sounds for people who had just lost all that they loved and who were facing an uncertain future. One thing we did know: that what lay ahead was suffering and pain before we would meet our long-awaited death. We were loaded into some of the wagons which had brought us here, but now only seventy were packed into each, for we were now "workers," not criminals, according to the Hitlerian terminology.

My body left Treblinka but Treblinka has remained deeply engraved in my heart and soul, and I shall never forget it to the day I die. Nor should the world ever forget Treblinka.

$\mathcal{J}ust$ those two words are enough still today, so many years after experiencing them, to rob me of my sleep.

Why did the Germans select a number of us, among those condemned to death, for a taste of Majdanek before dying? I cannot

Between Treblinka and Majdanek

explain it. Yet it is a fact that we were taken to Majdanek. We did not know this of course, at the time, but we knew intuitively that what lay ahead would not be kind.

We were given nothing to eat or drink in the trains, which further depressed our spirits. We had boarded the trains with heavy hearts. We had spent only several hours in Treblinka but had lived through so much, enough to last a whole lifetime for more than one man. We had left the ashes and bones of our families there and were now being led into another unknown world of evil.

An argument broke out in the trains at my suggestion to say Kaddish. Some said that as long as one does not know for sure, that one has not witnessed with one's own eyes the death of one's relatives, one must not say Kaddish, according to the law. The majority were of the opinion that what we did see was more than enough evidence of what the Germans were doing with us. We all recited the sad plaintive Kaddish for our loved ones, our friends, Klal Yisrael. It is difficult to capture in words the mournful lament of that painful Kaddish.

The train was traveling back in the direction of Warsaw. There are always optimists who immediately find a reason and an explanation for everything and in this way bolster their spiritual and maybe also their physical well-being. They argued that we were being taken to Warsaw to clear up the ruins and to bury the corpses. (The Germans indeed did bring Greek Jews for that purpose.) In the familiar Warsaw Ghetto we felt we could find a way out. A spark of hope surged up in us, but the hunger pangs and our overwhelming thirst brought us back to despair, particularly when the likelihood of returning to Warsaw waned.

Now a plan to escape arose. True, we knew from experience that the chances of survival were slim, yet....

The strongest supporter of escape was an engineer from Warsaw, who lived with a Gentile woman on the Aryan side. By accident, near the Jerusalem lanes, he fell into the hands of the Polish police who delivered him to the Gestapo and from there through the Umschlagplatz to Treblinka, and then he became one of our five hundred and seven. He was the first to jump when night came. He survived the jump but what happened to him later I do not know. Others tried but with less luck.

My friend Szymanowski suggested we jump together and go into hiding with some Gentile acquaintances. I did not want to save my life. This morning I had been a husband and father. Why should I fight for a life that was now meaningless — why endure all these agonies? I decided to leave my life to fate, to God's will. It was all one to me. I did not talk Szymanowski out of his plan but I simply said I felt no desire to join him. He understood my somber mood and also remained in the train. The inner struggles in our souls lasted for two days. I bewailed my fate all night. My balance sheet was complete. How long can a broken man like myself last? The end must come soon, so let destiny take its course.

In the morning, our thoughts turned to means of getting water. At a station we asked a Polish railway employee for some but he refused, claiming that the Ukrainians would punish him. We saw other railway workers and begged one for a piece of bread. For a pair of trousers he brought us a white roll. The heat was suffocating, our thirst intolerable, so we gave everything we had to our brothers, the Poles, in exchange for some water. They simply took advantage of us and cheated us. We suffered for seventy-four hours in the train and wished we would die, but what lay in store for us was worse than death. Just the name Majdanek was enough for a man's heartbeat to stop.

In the Torture Camp, Majdanek

One usually mentions Majdanek in one breath with Treblinka but there is a significant difference. Treblinka was a death camp only. The people lasted merely a few hours there, but Majdanek, which destroyed so many people, tortured its victims for weeks and months before killing them. There the soul was deadened first, then the body destroyed. Human beings lost every vestige of humanity. The cruelest sadists used the most refined and sophisticated tortures.

The train pulled up on a side-track. We waited for an hour for the SS guards, hundreds of them, rifles at the ready, to let us out of the trains. We got out filthy, exhausted and starved and had to line up to be counted. The count was thirty-seven short, representing those who had jumped. The Germans were very annoyed; this was not allowed to happen. In Majdanek the count must always be correct. The Ukrainians were admonished, but, as usual, the anger of the SS was aimed at us. It made no difference. Their plan to torture us was determined in advance.

We marched for several kilometers. On the way, we saw Jewish men working and Jewish women doing some laundering. These had volunteered for work and were given somewhat better conditions. They were not the inmates of the actual concentration camp. We were considered criminals, insurgents. Our most pressing concern now was to hide that which we had so far successfully salvaged. My friend had a little money. I had some jewelry hidden in a small 'honey box' which my son had given me in his last minutes.

We were stopped in a small clearing in front of the camp and were told we would be given soup in half an hour. A team of barbers, ordered to cut our hair, arrived. They explained that we would be undressed, sent in for showers, and then be given other clothes. Some took to swallowing five and ten ruble gold coins. Some attached valuables to the soles of their feet with band-aids. Some of us buried our treasures. We tried to make a deal with the barbers: we would entrust all our precious belongings to them, later to be shared with them. Whatever we tried did not succeed. As soon as we moved off that clearing, the soil was dug up.

We were subjected to a horrible examination; even our anuses were checked. Nor did the Czech Jewish barbers return our valuables. Moreover, on one occasion, when I attempted to win one of them over, he yelled at me so much that a German guard came up and gave me a violent beating. Those who had swallowed the gold coins later had to take the block-elders into their confidence, and that was fresh cause for torture and blackmail.

We were led into the bathhouse in groups and led out from another door so we could not recover anything we might have hidden. We were disinfected in a wooden bath with a chemical substance that attacked the skin and was particularly painful on any open wounds. We were each given clothing which was either too big or too small, and hats either the wrong size or belonging to women. We looked like clowns. We were all numbered and marked, the initials K.L. (*Koncentrazion Lager* — concentration camp) were painted on our backs and trousers. The Jews had to wear a yellow star. We had a tin number dangling around our necks.

In the yard, we met many inmates we knew. Many were working in the registration offices. They served loyally, sometimes a little too loyally, at the expense of their own brother Jews, in whose place they might easily have been. Each promised some help, such as an extra serving of soup, which for us was a promise of idyllic bliss. I was assigned to Block 22 on the third field. Our whole transport was assembled there to be initiated as camp inmates.

On that very first day in Majdanek, we began a search for those who had denounced the whereabouts of the bunkers, or those who had collaborated with the Germans. There were a few inmates in Majdanek — the block-elders of barracks six and seven — who executed retribution, bloodily settling accounts with the informers. The one in charge of my block was a character by the name of Heniek Kulik, the son-in-law of a reputable family in Warsaw, the tailor Nissan, who in turn was the Mendzickis' son-in-law. That scoundrel addressed us in language fit for the gutter, cursed us with the crudest Russian expressions to prepare us for camp life. He told us that here one only knows the time of one's arrival; the time of one's disappearance, no one knows. Here in this camp, we must submit not only to the will of the Germans but also to his will and fulfill whatever duty he imposes.

He used to run in constantly (for the first three days we were locked up) and call us to attention. That was his way of disciplining us. Also, the Germans kept coming in and we trembled in fear. They would watch us and search one or the other of the inmates. If they found anything, the miserable culprit would be given twenty-five lashes on his bare body. After three days, we were led out into the field, where we stood from early morning until twelve o'clock noon. We had to stand in rows of four. A thug by the name of Sova was chosen to train us. He did his job so well for his little extra soup that he was awarded an armband, and only then did he show himself in his true colors.

Roll call was a terrible ordeal. We were lined up out there an hour ahead, each block standing with its block-elder. The third field comprised twenty-two blocks, each group standing apart. When the SS, accompanied by the camp commander, passed by, counting, everyone stood in deadly silence. Every head had to be turned towards them like soldiers when parading past high military officials.

If anyone was missing, it was a day of mourning. The camp commandant would arrive with his officers and a search would begin. It once happened that an inmate fell asleep under a bunk. When he was found, he was hanged before our eyes. The camp commandant delivered a speech about the frivolity of the inmate who overlooked the hour of roll call. On another occasion, a young man fainted in the toilet and missed roll call. One thousand SS with tracking dogs searched Lublin for him. They found him two hours later still in an unconscious state. They hanged him and we had to stand and watch until 9:30 at night without a moment's respite. After such a roll call we returned to the barrack, a veritable stable for horses. It stank like a cesspool. At night we were not allowed out; two inmates were in charge of buckets, which we used in the dark. We were suffering from dysentery. All night we ran to the buckets, queued up or if we could not wait, simply defecated on the spot, on the floor. Those who had their bunks close by wished they would die.

These recent events had completely demoralized me. The pain and my thoughts kept me awake. It occurred to me that the name Kulik was familiar to me. I asked him on the following day whether Eliasz and Yuzek Zweier were his uncles. We discussed his family whom I knew well, upon which he asked me for money, not for himself, God forbid, but for the Kapos, for cigarettes. I told him that some had been taken away in the bathhouse, some I had buried, but did not know whether it was still there. At that, he walked off, ignoring my assurances that I had money on the Aryan side. He went looking for other victims. For the promise of a little soup, he found informers who would eavesdrop on conversations and denounce anyone who had any money. The barrack supervisor insisted that the money be given to him. When anyone refused, he was given fifty lashes.

One of the Kapos, Bobi, was a particularly well-known looter of money and a blackguard. He was only fifteen but looked like a grown man. That scoundrel was a fine example of German indoctrination. He had come to Majdanek with his parents and, in order to find favor with the Germans, personally hanged them at the Germans' request. His methods of torturing could lead one to his death in just a few minutes. Bobi beat me, but I had no money. He then left me alone. He would always visit the camp elders, looking for people to persecute.

A few days later I saw a new face, that of Numek Nissan — Heniek Kulik's brother-in-law — also a policeman. In Warsaw, he had been my client and we had always enjoyed a friendly relationship. Here he had the job of sharing out the soup. I asked him for a little extra. He swore at me, telling me that here I was a nobody, not the merchant I had been in Warsaw. Here, he said, things were different. Here it was K.L. (Kein Leben — no life) and ordered me to get out of his sight. Circumstances certainly affected changes in people. It was clear to me that I would perish under such conditions but I accepted my fate with equanimity. I had not yet developed the strength to bear the pain. Yet man can overcome everything.

In that human darkness and among humans transformed into animals, I did meet up with one very beautiful human being, a fine young man from Lodz, Akavia, learned and sensitive. He worked in Barrack 11 with the Cantor Sherman, Dr. Zadzewicz, and the brothers Schein. Akavia procured me a little soup, a piece of beetroot. He also asked my acquaintances to help me. Dr. Zadzewicz once brought me a bowl of soup in the middle of the night after finishing his shift. Genuinely fine human beings are not affected significantly by conditions in a concentration camp. And now, a new spate of ordeals was beginning for me. A new supervisor by the name of Osfiss, another of Kulik's brothers-in-law, joined us, who even surpassed the other two in vulgarity and callousness. He dispatched any inmate without money to do the heaviest jobs and subjected them to agonizing hardships. He confiscated our bread rations and demanded cigarettes in exchange. He would serve us one-half liter instead of three quarters and sell the leftovers. We were completely at the mercy of these three brothers-in-law.

We reported the soup scandal to the kitchen. Osfiss was given a bloody flogging, and lived to take revenge on us. He organized night searches, embittered our already miserable lives. The three flogged us until their arms ached.

During the first days, we were put to work on the spot, performing totally unnecessary work aimed simply at causing us hardship. We were made to transport heavy rocks from one location to another and to push wheelbarrows with soil. Some, swollen with hunger, were sent to Block 19, supposedly a sick-bay, but in fact the transfer-point for the crematoria. Daily selections took place from our barrack to Block 19, to the ovens. Some requested to be transported to Block 19.

Later we worked in a quarry, under Kapos and supervisors, who were relieved of their posts and punished accordingly if they did not beat the workers effectively. One particularly windy day, I was ordered to collect scraps of paper, some of which were soon scattered by the wind. The Ukrainian guard ordered me to bend over and I was given fifteen lashes with a heavy stick. I asked why I was getting five additional lashes. My howls could have raised the dead. When I was pushing a wheelbarrow full of soil, a Ukrainian Kapo whipped my hands. I dared ask him why. He beat me around the head with an iron rod.

I was assigned to the road-building commando Strassebahn, under the supervision of Ukrainians and a few German Kapos. Among them was a Viennese criminal who had been sentenced to twelve years' jail for rape. We were eight hundred. The Viennese Kapo introduced a sadistic system of smothering six to eight people daily. He would pick on his victims, give them tasks they were not strong enough to fulfill, would then order each to step into a ditch, and would press his right foot on the victims throat until he died, unable to breathe.

We lived in constant terror. We made a decision not to report for work. The block elders relayed our action to the camp supervisor who simply ignored them and said that the Viennese criminal could dispose of us as he pleased. The barrack supervisors came up with the idea that he should be bought off with alcohol and cigarettes. We were forced to give up our bread rations twice weekly, out of our meager eighth of a loaf per day. But the scheme did not work. The barrack supervisors drank the alcohol themselves and the Viennese guard, when he did get some of it, took it as his due. Nothing changed. On the contrary, things got worse from day to day. We again told the supervisors we would not go out to work on the Strassebahn. That threat was fraught with consequences for the barrack supervisors as well, so they decided to take fifty men from each barrack to average out the number of victims.

My turn came. It was about 4:00 P.M. one afternoon. I was running like the others with the wheelbarrows. The Kapo stopped me and ordered me to take a particularly heavy one and to pull it on the double. I didn't pass the test. The barrow usually weighed eighty kilograms and one had to run three hundred meters. Three times I ran that distance, and on the fourth I collapsed. The Kapo led me to a ditch, ordered me to lie down on my left side, and he began smothering me with his boots. I was very conscious of what was going on: I saw death; I heard everything. Every few minutes my executioner would stop, smoke a cigarette, and call out, "You're still alive, you dog." And then he would renew his attack. I felt myself weakening, my mouth was contorted and foaming, I could not move my hands. I could not cry out. I still heard my workmates filling their barrows saying, "He's gone, Mittelberg." I was angry at the thought of dying an ignoble death, crushed by the dirty, murderous boots of that butcher. That was my last lucid thought.

I heard blurred voices, "...into the forest." A miracle had occurred. An alarm had rung out in the camp and the Kapo had to leave me in the ditch to assemble the inmates. Fellow inmates dragged me out, very surprised that I was still breathing. I was lucky, they said, to have any life left in me after that painful ordeal which had lasted one and three quarter hours.

We heard the signal for roll call and marched into the camp. The Kapo looked us over first and when he caught sight of me supported by two fellow inmates, he used his rubber covered iron rod to beat me around the head, "What, you're still alive!" He beat me and for fear of getting hurt, my two friends let go of me. To my good fortune, he was called away. I marched, blood streaming down my face. The SS guard at the gate did not even bat an eyelid at the sight of the flowing blood. Such sights were normal occurrences. We were the last to arrive and all were waiting. My barrack supervisor didn't recognize me so disfigured was I by the bashing I had received. I was advised not to report to the doctor because one never returned from the hospital barrack.

I had to nurse my wounds myself. The barrack secretary, Isaac Rembo, an ex-secretary of the Judenrat, was a decent man, luckily. He organized the roster in such a way as to enable me to remain in the field between the barracks. Each field had is function. There was a garbage commando, a feces commando, and so on. At first I worked in the garbage commando. When taking the garbage out the senior worker would count us and declare, "I, inmate such and such, am now taking out so much rubbish and so many inmates." Going out, the SS gave us a good beating. While disposing of the rubbish, the Kapos gave us another beating. This was the so-called "better" job.

In the late afternoon, we were ordered to carry rocks and jump like squirrels. The Kapos beat our heads and hands. The wild scene of an armed Kapo, with a heavy stick pursuing an exhausted and helpless inmate, beating him incessantly, was terrifying. The inmate was covered in blood.

I tried out various jobs, which Rembo gave me at my request, but in every job I hoped for an early death. A man with bones of iron and a skull of steel could not have endured. Each one of us was badly bruised. We had wounds on our heads, our faces, hands, and legs. There was no shoulder to cry on, no one to turn to. Wishing to give me a little support, Rembo put me in charge of twenty men who were to work in the field gathering straws, scattered instantly by the wind. As I remember, Majdanek was indeed a windy place; the wind blew all the time. The job was quite difficult, since one had to bend all the time, watched closely by an SS officer.

At a certain point, the SS officer called me over to inform me that the workers were performing poorly and that it was up to me to make them work harder by whipping them. If I would not take to my task more seriously he would settle the account with me. I was incapable of fulfilling this order. It is true that the inmates were not working hard, since the job of bending constantly was difficult, but how could I raise a hand against them. Their state of physical exhaustion did not permit them to work any faster.

I urged my friends to pay attention when the SS officer was looking in their direction and then make more hurried movements as if they were working fast, but that tactic had no success. Twice he called me and warned me that my time of reckoning would come. Indeed that did happen. The third time he called me, swearing at me for not beating the workers, he did not send me back to my job but led me to a tree where he ordered me to bend over and gave me ten lashes with such force and fury, that I didn't believe I would be able to stand up again. He immediately replaced me with another supervisor who knew only too well how to carry out his orders. That is how my position of responsibility came to an end.

I had to beg Rembo to let me recover for at least two days; I was completely swollen and could hardly walk. Rembo appointed me to carry the water for washing the floors. In one of the fields, I met a Jewish young man who had already been in for a long time. He took me into his commando, where I worked until I left Majdanek. This in no way meant that I was spared beatings. The Germans, Poles, Ukrainians and Jews in positions of power saw to it that no one should go short of beatings, our daily bread.

My new job brought me to all five fields. It happened that on the fifth field, where the women were, I heard news of my sister. Akavia's daughter and other women, neighbors, told me that my sister, one of her children, and my two sisters-in-law had been there. The men had been sent to Poniatov. They had been sent away the day before. I had been unlucky and had just missed them. There was a rumor that all mothers and children had been summoned to report, an order the mothers had well understood and they accompanied their children on their last journey.

I was tired of living, not only because of my own troubles, but also because of what I saw around me. The saying that troubles shared are troubles halved did not seem quite true. I met one of my party friends, Menachem Plachte, a reputable merchant. He was beyond recognition. He was at the head of the Scheisse commando. On a certain day, for no apparent reason, (the Germans never lacked reasons) the commando was called and given twenty-five lashes each. Menachem Plachte didn't survive.

I met other acquaintances. My one-time accountant, Pinchas Marmelstein, Chaim Yosef Apfelbaum (he survived), Katz, Goldberg, Rosenwein, Weinstein, and others. My accidental meeting with Dr. Schiffer was a painful experience. He worked in the kitchen peeling potatoes, and was housed in the eighth block. On one occasion, he went out rather late from the block to go to work.

He was walking with another person, said in the camp to be his son-in-law — a fact I cannot establish for sure.

But to his misfortune, he met Bobi and the camp elder. The two thugs had gone out for a bit of entertainment and perhaps a little loot. They stopped and searched each person they met and woe to him who had not only a little money on him, but any item, particularly a pen knife, a spoon, or even a piece of paper. Camp inmates were forbidden to carry anything. For disobeying that order the culprit was either punished or put to death. I saw that they found some paper and, what was worse, a knife when searching Dr. Schiffer. At work he was allowed a knife as a potato peeler, and was supposed to return it at the end of the day. Since he probably had a good knife, he had considered it a pity to return it: a good knife made the work much easier. Bobi and the camp elder flogged him mercilessly, forced him to get up, and continued flogging him. At that point our commando left, and I was not able to see what happened further.

When I returned from work, I found out that Dr. Schiffer had died of a heart attack; that is how one of the finest leaders of our people, a learned man and a researcher, died at the hands of murderers.

My close neighbor who lived at 34 Rusfulna Street, Zinger, died in the nineteenth block. There was no end to our troubles. When we came back from work, I received my eighth of a loaf of bread and some colored water, which was supposed to be coffee and I lay down on the stone floor.

It is then that our own Jewish Hitlerite servants exhibited their skills: Kulik, Osfiss and Nissan. They woke us in the middle of the night and listed the crimes each one of us had committed. This one had relieved himself incorrectly, (pardon my vulgarity); that one had spat; that one had sewn on his number wrongly — and other crimes of this sort. For these wrongdoings each received ten, fifteen, and even twenty lashes. The Germans did not perform all the torture themselves; they also trained their servants. For example, they stationed a Russian armed with a heavy stick near the toilet to beat each person who entered. We were allowed very little time to go to the toilet, but this Russian beat us.

In addition to these troubles, the Kapos, Germans, and Poles alike demanded that we sing from morning until night. Every march was accompanied with singing and beatings; for not walking in step as the Kapo ordered, one received blows. There were great arguments with those who, not being strong enough to lift their feet, were constantly out of step. Others were afraid that because of them they would also be beaten. People swore at each other and even beat each other. We used to sing folk tunes about a Rebbe or Psalms, mostly Kol Nidrei. We chose Psalms of lament because they expressed our mood.

When we got back to our block we had to stand at attention in the rain and cold, naked, barefoot for hours. In order to warm ourselves, we attempted to turn our shoulders back to back, or to do some exercises, touching our toes. We had no luck. When we were lying in the bunkers or being taken in the wagons on the twelfth of May, it was very hot. Now, at the end of May the weather was very cold. Standing like that, trying to huddle up to one another, we looked rather like a flock of sheep than human beings. The women also had to stand like this on some occasions. Even when it rained we were not allowed to go inside, and we could pay with our lives for disobeying.

We suffered like this for months, and who knows whether we would have survived it, or if we would not have become totally animalized had a miracle not occurred. On a certain day we found out that a high-ranking officer had come to select strong, healthy men for all kinds of jobs. Locksmiths, shoemakers, bakers, tailors, metal workers were required. This was enough for us to begin dreaming again. Our hearts filled with joy and hope. The next day it was announced that we could register for work, each in his own trade. I registered as a baker, hoping that in a bakery I might have enough bread to satisfy my hunger. Only a thousand names were accepted.

It was only later that we discovered that there was some risk involved in applying for work. One fine morning a panel of doctors arrived to perform medical examinations. We were all assembled in the yard adjoining Block 19. We knew exactly what that could mean: life or death. The doctor didn't examine everyone. He simply picked the strong ones by their appearance, examined the weak ones, and sent them to Block 19. The selection went quickly. He did not examine me, and placed me among those who could still be productive. My neighbor, Zinger, had swelled up a few days before and was immediately sent to Block 19. After the selection, we were interned in specially allocated barracks.

We managed to say farewell to our friends from a distance. A new exact list was drawn up. The Kapos had decided to say farewell us in their own very special way. They got drunk and came in at night to impress upon us what Majdanek was. Even while we were eating, they beat us. Fortunately it was the last day. We were given clogs and clothing. We washed and walked to the train the next day. But where we were being sent no one knew.

Five hundred men were selected. The train was traveling at great speed. We arrived on the very same day in Skarziska, at the "Hassag" factory. We were divided into three groups. I was sent to work in workshop number 3C, an ammunition factory. It was my luck to have been picked for that workshop which had the worst conditions of the three and the hardest work.

Work for the Hungry Ones

At night, when we walked into the barrack, we found a group of Jews with a Jewish camp commandant, Jewish police, some

Jewish supervisors, and Jewish quartermasters. The camp came to life with our arrival. They asked us all sorts of things and we chatted. When they heard that we possessed nothing worth having after all our experiences, they lost interest in us. Yet we had one item with which to interest them. In exchange for a piece of bread we gave away our clothing. Theirs were full of holes burnt through by the chemicals they were handling in their work. For a small piece of bread they took a pair of pants and threw in their own threadbare clothes.

On the following morning, we were led to work. We walked quite a distance in our wooden clogs, until we reached a large factory with train tracks and bunkers. The whole area was carpeted with flowers and grass. On the surface it looked quite beautiful, but under the beautiful grass were the remains of many human beings who had died or been shot. Dr. Rast, the supervisor of the factory, came up to us. It was he who had brought us from Majdanek. It now became clear that registering us for work according to specific trades had simply been a ploy for getting us here. All the Germans required were strong people for absolutely useless work. The supervisors of each section came out to pick their own workers. The Germans were in charge and the Poles were their deputies. Dr. Rast himself picked those who would work on transport. I was shocked by the pasty color of the factory workers' faces. It was terrible to look at them. I, therefore, preferred to work on the transport.

I had another consideration in mind: in case we would be handling food, I would benefit. Of course, it turned out that there was no advantage to either of the work places. Death was everywhere. Every factory or storeroom was a cemetery. I was picked for the train transport and we began working almost immediately, loading grenades onto the wagons. It was Sunday, and the Polish supervisors worked us hard because they wanted to finish work as early as possible. It was our first day and we had no idea how to perform the task. We feared a grenade might explode and the Germans were concerned that we should, God forbid, not scratch any of them.

There were forty of us loading twenty wagons. A heavy shell could weigh up to fifty-two kilograms and we had to pass it from hand to hand. Besides that, there were some chemicals to be transported to a concealed bunker, inaccessible by van; therefore, the box had to be taken into the bunker on one's back. We found the job, supposedly a stroke of good luck, difficult. A wagon could take up to a thousand shells. Our strength was quickly sapped standing all day performing that dangerous and difficult task. Indeed, it proved too much for many to endure.

A great deal of difference existed between those of us who had just arrived from Warsaw and those who had come from the nearby small towns. We had arrived after the uprising in Warsaw, after Treblinka and Majdanek, and the others had come directly from their homes, still in possession of valuable items they were hiding. Besides, they still received help for a long time from the Judenrat which were close by. Also, the Gentiles with whom they had left their belongings used to help them from time to time. It was, therefore, much more difficult for us. The inmates resorted to stealing hunks of bread from each other, or an additional bowl of soup in the kitchen. If someone was caught he had a lot to answer for. One young eighteen-year-old got such a flogging from the cook that he died. One of our group, called Meir, constantly stole food from the kitchen. The blows he received did not frighten him or put him off; his hunger was greater than his fear.

The Jews who had arrived from the provinces ahead of us held all the service posts. Therefore a kind of antagonism grew up between them and those from Warsaw; among us, many refugees from Lodz. Let me record a few names at this point. The commandant Mordechai, a butcher by trade, had bought off the chief, thus achieving complete jurisdiction over us, which he knew exactly how to exercise. He released whoever had money from the drudgery of work. When I asked him for an exemption, he simply laughed. He disliked us intensely. He did not care whether someone was really ill. For money, he let his good friends go home and we had to work on their behalf. The tailor who made his garments was exempt from work. The same applied to the shoemakers. Wagons of shoes would arrive from Treblinka for distribution. Mordechai would then order the shoemakers to take the shoes apart looking for hidden wealth. They would keep the shoes that were in better condition, and pass the rubbish on to us.

The doctor also would issue an exemption for money; without money, one was obliged to go to work, regardless of the state of his health. After fifteen months of loading shells, I fell ill. On my way from work to camp, I had a very painful attack and could not walk. My friends supported me. Lenczner, a Jewish policeman from Volbram, noticed it and admonished me for not walking in the ranks. My complaints simply went unheard. He continued to kick me in the spine with his heavy boot in the very spot which was causing me the most pain. He tortured me the whole way. He survived the war. When I reached camp, I lay down and covered myself with a sheet of paper. My groans of pain kept everyone awake. In the morning, the whole business began again with the policemen forcing me to go to work.

After much haggling Dr. Rotbalsam came and, for money of course, gave me some ointment. All he wanted was money. He also survived. Mordechai had an assistant in our barrack by the name of Bakalasz. He refused to help anyone with anything. When I made any request of him, he would reply, "Ah, you'll die soon, so many people are dying, you'll also be among them." Mordechai had several other assistants, among them the brothers Avram and

Hershel Band of the same town, Volbram. Mordechai later died while attempting to escape. There were also the brothers Moishe and Kalman Gastfreund, tailors by trade. They were bad people. For forty days I lay in great pain, after which I was considered a convalescent, that is, I was sent to do easier work.

There were other thugs such as Dafner and Heinak. For spilling a little coffee they beat me so, that I was swollen for two weeks. They could have taught the SS officers a thing or two about how to perform beatings. There was a man from Crakow, Gershon Lesman; he and his two brothers had a lot of money, so they lived well. For five hundred zlotys he became a policeman.

When I worked at passing turf over the wire fence, I once opened the gate for the people of my group to come into camp. Lessman punished me for that by kicking me with the tip of his boot, inflicting excruciating pain in my back. I suffered another attack. Lesman is still alive and became very rich after the war. I have listed a number of those unpleasant characters.

So strong was the antagonism that the "veteran" inmates informed on the newcomers, refused to work with us, and so on. They used to talk of seven people and twenty newcomers having died on any given day. However, there was such a discrepancy between the death rate of the old timers and the later arrivals that soon the antagonism petered out. Every day forty people died. Of our group, which had numbered eighty, only seven remained at the end.

When the Germans realized that the mortality rate was threatening the numbers for work, they doubled our bread ration. True, the bread was not really bread, but a mixture of oats with — who knows — what else. The soups were made of tinned beetroots or cabbage. Once or twice a week we were given sweet soups, the answer to everyone's dream, the most gourmet delicacy. Very occasionally we were also given a teaspoon of marmalade. Right at the end we received a piece of very coarse sausage once a week. Whoever did not work on any particular day received nothing. The Poles also caused us plenty of trouble. It is true that we did not resent it quite as much as that coming from our Jewish persecutors. Nevertheless, we got our fair share of beatings and blows from the Polish guards. The "strong man" from storeroom three would torment an inmate he had selected for this purpose and not let him go before he had drawn blood.

The main sadist was Szevchik. Kovalik, Svedlo, Polenka the cook, and Zazicki were also quite effective. These guys were all very "in" and on the best terms with the commander Mordechai and his henchmen.

I saw that survival in this atmosphere was not going to be easy, so I began to think of trading as others did. But the others had money. It occurred to me to pull out my golden teeth with plain pliers, just as one tears off a piece of rubber. In this way, I soon accumulated a few hundred zlotys to buy myself something to eat. Szevchick, the Polish guard, traded in bread. He forced us to buy bread from him at fourteen zlotys, when we could have bought it for eight elsewhere. He was a vindictive scoundrel and would flog us with whips that cut into our flesh. All the while, he and Polenka sermonized that we Jews, having been well off in earlier days, had to suffer now.

In 1944, the request for shells increased and we were made to work eighteen to twenty hours a day, sometimes in a twenty degree frost without rest. After a day of hard work, when we lay down on our narrow bunks, the Germans came and dragged us out to work again; thirty-six wagons had arrived which we had to load up and return directly.

The Polish supervisors let their anger out at us. Some of the inmates hid out in the boiler rooms, so we had to work for them as well. The commander Mordechai took his protégés and went home, so we had to work for all of them. I was the victim. I worked all night, rested a few hours in the afternoon and then back to work. We were beaten so much that many simply collapsed and died. Walking back to camp, we still had to sing. This was the good fortune of being in a work camp. Starabinski, the leader of the Keren Hayesod in Warsaw and Shapiro, another Zionist leader from Lodz, died of typhus. In May 1944, the Germans began to prepare for evacuation. Later, it became clear that it had been too soon. Meanwhile, on a particular Sunday, everyone was ordered to register and to assemble for roll call.

A selection was carried out in the yard: the weaker ones were picked out and led to be shot. A girl who would not let go of her mother was shot on the spot. From that day on the agony of life or death began again. The process of selection was a nightmare. A few took place at which the Ukrainians, under the supervision of the Germans, carried out the executions. Following the selections, the Germans took to transporting people to unknown destinations. We were scared. The Germans kept only a nucleus of inmates to liquidate the camp and the rest were sent away. The Red Army, on which our hopes were pinned, was approaching. We worked day and night liquidating the camp until a certain morning when we were called away from work. A spark of hope arose in us that the Soviet army was close and that we were to be liberated, but our hopes were soon dashed. We were ordered to pack and prepare for a journey. Abram, the camp commander at the time, gave us bread and we left for the train.

Ukrainians were awaiting us to pack us onto open coal wagons. We drove around to the other workshops and collected all the others. All told, there were about a thousand of us. Each one had large parcels consisting of their own things, accumulated through the years, and of belongings of dead friends. From earlier experience, we feared that we would be shot underway.

The fear of being shot during this journey just prior to the impending liberation was obsessive. We had gone through so much and had survived, that we did not want to die now when the sun had begun to rise.

Hovering Between Life and Death Once Again

There were a thousand of us from all the workshops, surrounded by all our belongings, too precious to leave behind, but we had no knowledge of where we were being taken. We arrived in Piotrkow at 10:00 P.M. The SS were there to meet us, their guns cocked, and they began to harass us. We thought they were planning to execute us. Everyone threw down whatever they were carrying. After an hour of torment the Germans led us to the big Piotrkow prison, and there, in the prison yard, we all thought we were being led to our execution. A doctor even committed suicide. In the prison yard, we were given water from a hose. After a night spent in the yard, we were taken to the queue for Suleyuv. From the wagons, again we were taken to a stable for horses, filthier now than before, as it was full of lice and worms. We were given no food and only after a few days were tents set up for the Polish inmates, from whom we could sometimes obtain something to eat. But the Germans very quickly put a stop to that. They put up a wire fence to separate the Jewish prisoners from the Aryan ones. There were several thousand Poles from Warsaw and we had to build barracks for them.

We worked at eight to ten kilometers from the stable, a distance we were forced to cover on the run, particularly the last group of twenty-four such groups, which, without any reason, had been branded as unwilling to work. That group had to cover the distance in "Laufschritte" (at a running pace). Any prisoner who did not run well was beaten. One of the assistants beat me so long that my lip split, and he threw me into the water. What was our task? We were actually covering up the retreat of the German army.

In the forest we chopped down trees, spreading them on the water to slow down the advance of the Soviet Army. I worked in a commando that was laying mines. The hardest job, to be carried out with precision, was digging defense ditches. Each ditch had to be 6.5 meters by 3.5 meters. The forty groups of twenty-five men were busy digging ditches. If one hit on soft ground, it was easier, but in most cases the ground was hard. The representatives of the Todd Company walked around administering blows. Those who were unable to conclude the job in time remained until late and were beaten some more. They had to cover the return journey to camp in "Laufschritte."

It was not an easy thing to run for ten kilometers in the state we were in. I also had the misfortune of belonging to the penalty group. To aggravate matters we had the remnants of the Ghetto, the Jewish police, with us here also. They were the leaders and aggravated our already desperate plight.

Dr. Zaks, a native of Crakow whom we had the misfortune of knowing in the Skarzisker Workshop A, followed us to this new camp and also here he applied the same methods as he had in the workshop. He declared all the sick, the elderly and the weak as being fit for work, thereby contributing to their death, for, as they could not carry out the work satisfactorily, the Ukrainians and Germans wore them out and beat them to death.

Arriving back after work, we were given a little watery soup and lay down on the naked ground without any covering. The rain poured in on us and many developed pneumonia. We worked for four weeks in these totally inhuman conditions, but this also came to an end.

On a certain day we were broken up into two groups of five hundred. One group was immediately transported, as we later discovered, to Czestechow. The fear of any change was so strong that each person made every effort to be the last to leave, in case the

Soviet army would arrive. But the other group, to which I belonged, was also led away to the wagons on the following morning at 6:00 A.M. We immediately noticed that our Ukrainians were not with us, only SS. We understood that we were setting out on another journey of torture to Germany. The wagons were closed ones, for cattle of course. The wagon was divided in two, twenty-five people in each half and the SS were guarding us in the reserved center section. They advised us to buy food, since money would be useless. Of course we mistrusted them for we knew that they would take away an unfair share of our food purchases. But this time the ones who did take up the suggestion did well. We bought bread and fruit. We consoled ourselves that the Germans would also be hungry.

The kilogram of preserved meat that the Germans gave us in addition to our bread ration was inedible. Many people suffered food poisoning and terrible stomach cramps. The SS placed a bucket in each wagon. At night they left the wagon, locking it from the outside; it was then that the real fun began.

We all had diarrhea; the buckets spilled over on the floor. People started fighting one another and were rolling in the slime. There was a policeman in our wagon by the name of Korn, who had already harassed us in Silev and continued to beat us with his spurs here in the train. I resented his behavior deeply and interfered in the fight for which, of course, I got my share of blows. That fellow, who had tormented us so, received his due in Buchenwald. The following morning we arrived in Buchenwald. The stench in the wagon was such that, had we had to travel any further, we would not have survived.

Upon our arrival, we were greeted by a guard of honor of SS and entered through the fine entrance gates. Inside, we caught sight of people from various countries. There was a hum of a variety of languages. The one thing that reminded us of our common fate was the prison garb.

Light and Shade in "International" Buchenwald

We were lined up in the yard. A Jew approached us and held a speech in which he explained that everyone was equal here. The Jewish police would have absolutely no say over us. He told the policemen to remove their caps, no longer did they have any special status, and requested that we identify those who had tormented us. The policemen blanched, begging for mercy, but their pleas went unheeded. The following men received their just sentences in Buchenwald: A German Jewish policeman, Korn, whom I mentioned earlier. It happened as follows: Early one morning, the "old timers" in Buchenwald gave our persecutors from other camps a thorough beating. Later, the latter were put to death by some other means. Others who received their just sentence with Korn were Abram, from workshop three, Dr. Zaks whom I mentioned earlier, a policeman Alek from workshop three, and others. A Jewish policeman by the name of Tepperman also met his death in Buchenwald as well as a German camp leader Kinneman who, acting on Tepperman's advice, was responsible for the death of many Jews in Skarzisko. Shepicki also died in Buchenwald.

We were led to the bathhouse. As usual, this was an opportunity for stripping all newcomers of any remaining belongings including cigarettes. Most of those who had hidden cigarettes in their footwear managed to salvage them. A little tobacco represented a fortune in camp. Thanks to a few cigarettes, I myself was able to improve my situation a little. There were about forty thousand inmates in Buchenwald, among them many smokers. Particularly those who performed some official function could afford to trade food for cigarettes.

At night we stood at roll call. For the first time, we heard some humane words coming from the mouth of a German camp leader. A German socialist spoke to us and reminded us to keep together, to help one another, to practice a certain comradeship. He reassured us that we should not fear anything; we should speak about everything that bothers us. He advised whoever was ill to go immediately to see the doctors, warned us not to be afraid since Buchenwald had no crematoria. In short, this all seemed to us like a dream. As we were to find out later, many had paid with their lives to achieve this situation. Bitter fights with the SS and with the Kapos had been fought.

We worked in a quarry carting stones. On the whole, we felt reasonably well in Buchenwald. But the camp was only a central point used to redirect the train transports to various work camps. Only the young and weak remained in camp.

This idyllic state did not last long. Another work camp, Szliebin-Buchenwald 17, awaited us, who were experienced work hands. On a certain day we were all examined, weighed, and measured and each one of us received a number. I was then ill, but was nevertheless diagnosed by SS doctors as being still fit enough to work for German "victory". My number was 84577.

It was with much sadness that I left Buchenwald, a place that seemed like a paradise to me. In Szlebin we saw only desolate forests and newly-built barracks. We were, for the time being, a forest-commando. The supervisor was a good man but the young Nazi who led our commando was just as cruel and brutal as the ones we had encountered at other camps.

He would sit in the forest watching us collect twigs. He beat anyone who dared to rest for a moment after bending a thousand times. We reported not only the floggings but also his constant cursing at us. Our complaint cut no ice. It is true that this eighteen-year-old scoundrel was removed, but a criminal who had been sentenced to fifteen years' hard labor replaced him. He was, generally speaking, a fool and understood little. One thing he did extremely well, with most sophisticated methods, was torture people. We again complained, but to no avail.

In the meantime, we had been divided into various commandos for work in the ammunition factory. We were producing a kind of shell, a grenade.

I had the luck to belong to the commando called Lehman, which of course was the worst one. We worked twelve hours a day in two shifts. The factory consisted of four large rooms. Everyday we had to produce forty thousand grenades. Our Kapo was a very imaginative gypsy with a criminal past and an outstanding talent for inflicting physical pain. He woke us at 4:00 A.M. The sick and those who still were suffering from the lashings they had received simply could not put on their rags quickly enough without being beaten again. Our own supervisors, Aranowicz and Kivkowicz had not learned their lessons from Buchenwald and tortured us callously. During roll call, in rain and snow, we had to wait for the Kapo, sometimes for hours. Only then did we leave for work, but not before some other entertainment. At the gate, the SS played a game with us, "hats off." In a state of total exhaustion at the end of the day we headed back for the wooden barracks unheated.

Our job consisted of transferring pipes from various train tracks and fields onto so-called "platforms". Two people worked at one of these platforms. I worked with Moshe Klarfeld, a wonderful person. For some time, I also worked filling these pipes with certain chemicals. Gunpowder was inserted into the pipe, a cardboard stopper was placed at one end, and a detonator was attached on the side. It was with this kind of primitive ammunition that the Germans deceived themselves that they would withstand and overcome the allied forces.

Working with cold metal in bitter cold weather caused our fingers to freeze, and we could not fulfill our daily quota of ten thousand grenades. We were given very little to eat. The Kapo in charge and the Jewish block elder did not care to take these factors into consideration.

That little fellow with the loud voice, Aranowicz, and the scoundrel Kiwkowicz beat us mercilessly till our blood was flowing. That is how I remember our friend Meir, beaten up and covered in blood.

Of course I also got my share. One such attack by Kiwkowicz left me broken and suffering for weeks. In the meantime, our hunger became unbearable. Our only hope was that when a wagon of potatoes would arrive, we would steal a few for ourselves. But our Jewish camp supervisors, one by the name of Freifeld and another, could not tolerate to see us benefit and simply dispersed and beat us. Our screams came to the notice of the Untersturmfuhrer, who ordered that the whole camp be punished by having that day's total daily ration held back from us. More people began crowding around the rubbish bins. There was always a lot of traffic around there, but that day, it was particularly terrible. One would look for raw potato peels, rotten turnip peels, and the outside leaves of the cabbage, which we consumed on the spot.

There was another auspicious opportunity to obtain a little more food: to be in charge of transporting the food from the kitchen and to carry back the pots, a job which earned those doing it an extra bowl of soup. That meant a great deal. Four people (according to the roster) were required each day to carry the pots, which provided an opportunity to sustain us a little longer.

It was always a good idea to frequent the kitchen, just in case the cook would show a little pity. Those a little more daring and agile sometimes used to appropriate food from the storeroom. Others negotiated with the Germans if they still had something to sell.

Another means of obtaining some additional food was to go and work on the train tracks. The work was hard. We were to put stones between the tracks and then press them down with iron rollers. But, at least there was the opportunity to steal away into the fields and dig something up, perhaps a potato or a turnip peel.

I succeeded, through an exchange of cigarettes, to acquire some sugar. Together with another guy, we began manufacturing sweets and that is how I earned a little to buy more bread. It was all done of course at great risk and one sometimes endured losses as in any other risky business.

Life for our Untersturmfuhrer was very jolly. Thanks to us he had not been called to the battlefront and he had a comfortable livelihood in addition. He felt happy so he ordered us to sing. He was very musical and forced us to sing while marching to and from work. A musician taught us some songs, which we rehearsed at specially arranged times. We also had special days set aside for singing, naturally, Sundays. Our repertoire consisted of *Drei Lilien* — "Three Lillies" and *In Einem Kleinen Polnisch Statchen* — "In a Small Polish Village."

It is worth noting that the Germans remained true to their culture even in this. If someone sang a false note or did not join in the singing, he was singled out and handed over to the Kapos. Who knows how long this cultural aspect to our affliction would have lasted, if not for the explosion in the camp. Only then did the Untersturmfuhrer forget about educating us.

It happened in the middle of the night. The glass panes fell out and the barracks collapsed. We ran outside stark naked. In the distance we caught sight of a huge fire in the direction of the factory.

We also saw people running out of other barracks. In this total turmoil, no one knew what to do. The SS ordered us to hide in the bunkers; some ran into town. What emerged was that the allies had actually bombarded the factory and had hit the target with precision. The boilers immediately burst into flames. Those who had been on shifts had of course been killed. It could have been us! Dead bodies were brought in, some without limbs or other members of their bodies. The fire raged for another twenty-four hours. The survivors were called to a roll call, and we now heard that, in the confusion, some of the inmates had ransacked the barracks and robbed the Kapos' and the block elders' possessions. We were searched at roll call and four inmates were found with stolen goods, (among them Shternzisz). The bandits took the four, stripped them of their clothes, tied them to a tree and gave them a brutal whipping.

A special SS commission came after the fire to investigate the situation and the causes of the explosion. It was also their duty to reconstruct the factory. On Sunday, we were made to stand in the yard and one of the most callous Kapos, a gypsy, welcomed us with the following words, "You know me no doubt. I was in Auschwitz and I finished you off there. I'll do the same here also if you won't want to work."

We were again divided into groups. Each group of twenty had to carry a track of one thousand kilograms while running rhythmically in time. In our weakened state it was difficult to execute these capricious requests. If the track seemed to them not completely straight, the young seventeen-to-twenty-year-old murderers beat us viciously. They would chase us and beat us. It looked like a tragic game, not at all like work. We saw not a ray of hope, our anguish was boundless and our torment did not stop at the close of the day.

We were then stripped naked in the cold and searched for pieces of blankets. French women working in a neighboring enclosure witnessed one such search. Their gentle faces were full of sympathy and pain. They wept, watching us suffer. I felt, then, that they were more than sisters to me.

The other commandos at the end of the day told us of their trials and tribulations. We believed that our agony would never come to an end. We swore to take unconditional revenge; that was our sole consolation.

We rebuilt the factory in several weeks. Meanwhile, the Soviet army was approaching and the Germans began building factories in other locations. Buchenwald provided the victims.

When the Red Army was at sixty kilometers from Szliebin, the factory was still functioning. During the liquidation of the factory we were working around the clock. All we heard was *"Weiter machen!"* "Continue to work!" Then we received a blow. That was our daily diet.

One evening when we got back to camp we were lined up and a list was read out of five hundred who were to go to Plasberg to build a factory there. We knew already what that entailed. Hence each one began begging the supervisors not to be included on the list, rather to be left where we were. That scoundrel Aranovic owed me seventy marks, so he was rather interested to get me out of the way and I was sent to a special block. Our supervisor there was an engineer by the name of Hartman.

All we got on the road was a pair of wooden clogs, and these were not provided out of charitable concerns. Plasberg was full of terrible swamps; also the Jewish leadership of the camp there was swampy, consisting of absolute outcasts and primitive people. We feared a death-camp, the camp we found was equally grim.

The camp guards, supported by their Jewish assistants, attacked us and robbed us of all we still owned. They took away my cigarettes and a pen knife which I still had managed to hide. Among those Jewish attackers, two stood out, Starowski from Kelc and Motele Salcman.

At night we lay down on the wet ground without cover. As we had expected, the work was not easy and our plight was aggravated by our supervisor, Dr. Hornung from Cracow. He survived, may his name and memory be effaced. We begged him to spare us at roll call, not to let us stand for hours in the cold for no purpose. But he simply laughed callously. The work was headed by the Leipziger SS. Each SS officer followed two inmates bearing a box of grenades or pipes. Anyone who tripped was beaten, and thousands met their death there.

Every morning, when work began, a car load of SS would arrive who began beating us the moment they touched ground. The Oberscharfuhrer would stand and laugh while taking notes, probably recording how many Jews each of those young thugs was beating. It is beyond my comprehension how such young people, so recently still under their mothers' influence could commit such murderous acts. Yet the Germans were capable of everything, just as it proved possible for us to endure such treatment.

There was also a sick bay under the supervision of the notorious Dr. Rotbalsam who did not assist the sick but used his position to improve his own lot.

Our SS supervisor was the Unterscharfuhrer Schmidt, whom we nicknamed "Tsik Tsak", due to the fact that he was always positioned at the gate with a whip in his hand, and beat us around our heads while singing "Zag Zag". He was in the habit of creeping up stealthily to catch anyone resting a little. He didn't always administer the punishment on the spot. He would note the number of the unfortunate victim who, in the evening, would be given fifteen or twenty lashes.

For a little tobacco and a gold tooth I had pulled out of my mouth, the German in charge of the storeroom, Neumeister, took me in to work there, but also there, an SS officer made life unbearable. The storeroom was next to the Italian kitchen and one could, every now and then, snatch an extra beetroot, or some other scrap of food, but my good fortune did not last long. The Szliebin camp commander arrived in Plasberg and immediately forbade all Jews to work in the storeroom.

When I made certain requests from the German who had taken my gold tooth, he provoked the Ukrainians onto me and I got a terrible beating. While carrying heavy gas pipes one day I noticed a turnip peel on the ground. I ran to pick it up, but as I bent down an SS appeared and beat me with a branch. I still suffer from a bad back today. The Germans learnt this trick from the Poles and Ukrainians who used to make a game of this. During lunchtime break, Jews would sneak up to the kitchen in the hope of finding something to eat, but the bandits were already waiting for them and would beat them. This was all happening right at the end of the war, when it was quite clear that the Germans would be defeated.

One evening we heard the alarm signals followed by bombings; the factory had been hit. Everything was destroyed. For us it signaled the beginning of more hard labor. We went on being chased and beaten. People were dropping off; illness was spreading. In a very short time, five hundred out of the one thousand three hundred inmates died. In place of those who had died a new group arrived from Grossrossen. Thirty days they had spent on that march, many had died on the way. We felt the offensive was reaching us, as discipline was becoming a little more relaxed. We were not being forced to work quite so hard. We had, of course, mixed feelings as a result. On one hand, we anticipated the approaching liberation and, on the other, we did not believe, knowing the Germans, that they would let us live to see that moment. Secretly, the Germans were preparing to abandon Plasberg. They ordered us to undress, to take off our coats which they appropriated, hoping we would die of cold. It was January, the bitterest cold of winter. Our block elder, Zeligman, from Lodz, carried out this particular act.

We also suffered from another plague, lice. We were being eaten alive. The Germans no longer paid any attention to hygiene and we suffered terribly. Maybe they intended us to die of bacterial warfare.

Time was moving on, meanwhile, but with no prospect of change. We were very desperate. People wanted a change, not thinking what that change might signify. It finally did come, when, one morning in 1945, we were ordered not to go out to work. Another order came to attend roll call. We all understood that we were being transported once again. We ran into the barracks to collect the few belongings, which, even in such poor conditions, a human being accumulates.

We took with us various items. I had two small containers of wheat, which the tailor Firestein had been minding for me. The Oberscharfuhrer "Tsik Tsak" attended by his henchmen, soon arrived to drive us into the wagons in a great hurry, without food of course, and without any explanation as to where we were being taken.

Only the electricians and their Kapo, Narciz, remained behind. We had believed, all along, that Narciz, a decent man, was a Gentile. The electricians enjoyed some privileges. It was they who carried the soups, yet they also went hungry.

In each wagon, seventy or eighty men were piled in. The wagon was small and dirty and of course we were hungry and were given nothing. Only on the third day of travel did we receive something to eat, and after that, nothing again. On the fourth day we saw, through the planks of the wagons, that we were standing in forests. No one recognized this spot. The SS were partying in their wagon. On the fifth day there were corpses in every wagon.

Dying had become a natural occurrence. When one does not eat, one must die. A few minutes earlier one might have been talking to a mate and then he stretched out and died.

We had to do something. We didn't want to expire of hunger like that, so in unison, we all began calling out "Bread, bread, shoot us!" but we achieved nothing. By the seventh day, forty were dying daily. Our transport numbered 1,247 men, among them also Russian, Rumanian, and Hungarian Jews. The latter showed very little endurance.

In our wagon there were three lively guys, the Bergman brothers. Together with another few, among them a Russian Jew who had an iron rod, they made a hole in the floor. They waited till the train slowed down a little and jumped out, first the Bergman brothers and the Russian, and then another twelve jumped. The first probably escaped safely; we heard no news of them.

We did hear what happened to the next dozen. They went, all twelve of them, weak and worn out, into the first hut they saw. They understood that it would have been wiser to seek help one at a time, but no one wanted to be the last. They could not communicate, as it was in Czechoslovakia. They were unshaven and looked unkempt. Their appearance didn't inspire anyone with confidence and the boys, hearing that these were Jews, informed the police. Eleven were caught and one managed to escape. They were led back to our wagons and there our tragedy began. Had "Tsik Tsak" seen a half-empty wagon, he would have punished us accordingly, but seeing that some had tried to escape he took to us with a vengeance. He stood us in a line and, not leaving anyone out, beat each with a heavy rod. That didn't seem to be enough so he went to fetch help. We thought maybe we had gotten rid of him. One of the captives took out a piece of carrot from his pocket which led to a fight between them. Meanwhile Tsik Tsak came back with a whole team and again took to flogging us. We had been through a great deal but now we thought we had indeed reached our end. The Hitlerian beast was in its death throes and we could still feel its teeth. We were being beaten with steel rods and some were killed. A guard came up to me, and recognizing me as the one who had tried to steal a turnip peel, called out to me, "Ah ha, this is the turnip thief. I'll beat you to death!" He took a piece of iron and gave it to me. Those blows have never left me. Besides that, they took those who had escaped out of the wagon and shot them. Ten were shot, the eleventh died of the beating.

When the corpses had been taken out we were once again packed into the wagon with hardly any room to sit. There were some resourceful people who used belts and their blankets to make a hammock and hung themselves above everyone in the wagon. One day we were let out of the wagons onto the field. We took to eating the leaves and grass like animals. We fell ill and some died. In the distance we saw closed wagons loaded with sugar. The SS appropriated the sugar and traded with us. I also gave in a few cigarettes but received no sugar in exchange.

So desperate were we that the thought of suicide became a serious consideration. And if not suicide, then a young man of twenty-three had a better idea, to attack the Germans and thereby die. While speaking to us thus, he noticed a train pass by and threw himself under it. The train amputated his leg. "Tsik Tsak" saw this from afar and, with dancing little steps, went up to the victim saying, "Suffer, you dog," and then threw stones into his open wound. The wounded man kept yelling to us to take revenge. He swore at the Germans and threw a stone at "Tsik Tsak" until the Germans dragged him away.

There was among us in the wagon a strong man, Shlome Stein. In camp he had been able to pick up an electric motor of over one hundred kilograms with one finger and now he was dying of hunger like a dove and was bidding me farewell. I do not know what would have happened to us if not for the Czechs. They tried with all possible means to get a piece of bread to us. More than once they came to "Tsik Tsak" and pleaded with him to leave us there to work, but he simply ignored them. Every morning he would inquire as to how many had died and he would always add, "Too few". We suffered like this for eighteen days, even relieving ourselves in those locked wagons.

On one occasion, the representatives of the Czech civil authorities didn't come alone, but they brought local SS and they requested two hundred men to clean up some damaged wagons. Although I had difficulty moving due to the beating I had received, I immediately volunteered. I begged my friend Sheinfeld to support me, for I could hardly walk. We saw some damaged wagons full of potatoes five hundred meters away. We wanted to run up quickly, but the SS did not allow us. Our work consisted of clearing the area of the broken-down equipment. Meanwhile, we caught sight of burnt turnips and we threw ourselves on them. The Czech who was accompanying us promised to give us potatoes at the end of the job. I could not collect any turnips, so my friend shared his with me.

There is a children's story about a little table, which fills with the best dishes, at the sound of magical bells. Such a magical bell we heard there. It was a signal which Czech women gave for us to stand in line while they distributed delicacies: white bread, cheese, sausage, and who can remember what else.

We were happy and overwhelmed and we were even more astonished when again, before leaving, we heard the magical bell and again we were offered these wonderful foods. This time we took part back for our friends. We also stuffed our pockets full of potatoes. A Czech organization had arranged this treat. The SS did not usually allow the Czech women to help us, so they had devised a ruse. On another occasion they asked for one hundred and fifty men for an hour's work and the SS could not refuse. I have no words for the Czechs. They restored my belief in man, in humanity. I took a bag with me and filled it with as many as ninety potatoes, I could not stop. Once back in the wagon, I collapsed and needed help. We shared our treasure with those who had been left behind, but they wept that they had not been the fortunate ones.

"Tsik Tsak" begrudged us our good fortune and we left that place back into hell without food and without water. Again we fought over the potato peels, but even more, we suffered from thirst. In vain I stood all night holding a small box out hoping for some raindrops but no rain fell.

On the way, we came across a transport of women in the same horrendous situation as we, but they had more stamina than we. The entire journey was a long drawn out cemetery. "Tsik Tsak" was simultaneously a murderer and a grave.

After eighteen days we arrived in a city, and were led into a new camp. We crawled out of the wagons with difficulty, some of us had to be laid out. Filthy, covered in lice, and without a human appearance, we arrived in the death camp Matthausen.

Light doesn't appear until total darkness has reigned. Liberation was very close. The Allied tanks could be heard already very close by but for us, captives, liberation was still distant and very unsure. No one felt confident that he would survive to see it, although the victory of the Allies was probable and almost all of Germany was occupied by Soviet or Allied forces. Indeed many of us did not have the good fortune to welcome freedom. In those last days great numbers of people perished. Also, for those who did survive, those last days were the most difficult.

The Last Stage

We suspected, and we were right, that the Germans would do

everything to annihilate us in order to wipe out all traces of what had taken place, but that was not the only reason. Evil is such a hypnotic force that the murderers practice it even at a time when logic tells them to change their tactics. This was particularly true of the sycophantic Jewish collaborators, who inflicted no less pain on us than the Germans had.

We had to help one another in order to alight from the high wagons, so weak were we. We were unable to walk. Some men were simply laid out alongside the tracks. In the fields we saw prisoners working, mostly Russians; they were digging potatoes. At our request they threw us some but again the SS put a stop to it.

Dragging our feet, we began the march up to Matthausen, situated on a hill like a fortress. Walking was a great effort. We kept falling. We just made it to the gate, which opened up wide to allow us in. We were left standing for a long time in the yard. Our eyes had become accustomed to search out the kitchen. No one worried that we should even receive some water. We began trading with the kitchen. The young boys took money for everything: for coffee, for a little bit of soup; bread was like gold. Also the camp SS were very skilled in camp trade, and cheated unashamedly. As soon as they received something in their hands they disappeared. We were left with no bread and no money. There were two brothers Szimonovich among us. They still had fifty dollars on them from their hometown, Czestochow, for which they now wanted to buy bread. They were careful enough and traded with the kitchen, they received the bread through the little window, but had not anticipated the effect that a loaf of bread would have on the inmates. Suddenly a wild throng attacked them with such impetus that it was hard to establish who had grabbed the bread, it simply disappeared. The brothers Szimonovich were left with not a crumb of it.

Seeing the total confusion, the cooks threw pieces of bread, as if to dogs, making a game of it, throwing a piece here to a pretty woman, there to a group where they expected to provoke a fight. Others, meanwhile, took over the rubbish bins and discovered a treasure, horse bones, which they sucked with such enjoyment as if they were the tastiest marrowbones, straight out of a *cholent*. Others begged them to pass on the bone when they had finished with it.

We spent a day and a night in the yard, lying on the naked stones under the open sky. Meanwhile all the inmates of the camp had assembled and found relatives. Some found a spouse; women who had thought that their husbands were dead and vice versa.

We were so hungry that one did not even envy the other the fact that they had found relatives. We only envied them the little food their relatives were able to give them. The camp leadership completely ignored food and drink but they did not overlook exercising us. They organized all kinds of tricks with us, starving, thirsty and exhausted as we were. They warned us that we would die anyway: "There is only one road here and it leads to death."

After a full twenty-four hours they relented and gave us a piece of bread. Of course one tries one's luck in a new situation and we ran to try and get another piece, but one received mostly blows instead of bread. After the food came the orders. We were told to undress. The clothes were removed by special teams for disinfection, but we never saw them again. We were very thoroughly searched and everything was taken away from us: pen knives, lighters and such like. They knew that after bathing we would be let out from the other side and would be left with nothing. Indeed they sold our things. Also the Jewish barbers beat us for not keeping our heads up. I don't know whether they were good barbers, I was not interested in an elegant haircut, but they were expert at giving out blows.

After the showers we were given underwear, and in that get-up, we paraded past the women into the barracks where we were stamped and registered.

Two thugs stood checking the underwear we had just received. They were looking for a possible louse and, of course, found one. Even if there were none they said there were and took away our underwear, leaving us naked. If we tried to protest we got beaten. I was petrified. This was worse than Majdanec. A minute earlier I had been a rich man, with some clothes on my back. Now I was naked and shivering with cold. I need not have worried about clothing, where they were sending us we needed no clothing. In the sick house to which we were assigned, the supervisors' only task was to finish us off as quickly as possible. At that time, there was some disorder in Matthausen among the Germans; no roll calls took place and the block leaders could go on claiming the bread of those who had died for some time after their death. So the supervisors did everything to hasten death. They thought up very sophisticated means of increasing the mortality rate.

One of the most horrifying chapters was sleeping on the bunks in the sick house in Matthausen. The board was sixty centimeters wide and five people lay on it: two on one side, two on the other and the fifth one on top. I was told to climb on top of one of these. When I got up, I saw a terrible picture. The patients had open weeping wounds, which gave out a terrible stench. The four, who were hardly alive, and lay in excruciating pain begged me not to add to their suffering. I went down again and tried to explain to the Jewish supervisors that there was no room up there for which I was given another beating, and, as punishment, I was made to lie on the concrete floor.

There were another ten victims lying in that corner cell. The block elders had already selected these as their next victims. The ten of us received one torn blanket, probably not to cover ourselves with but to fight over. After suffering through the night I dared go to the doctor, for which I was kept out in the cold for five hours. It was raining and snowing and I could not say a word without receiving an even greater punishment. After that experience, the concrete floor seemed like a warm home. Those sharing the floor with me were dying one after another. That is what the block guards were waiting for. One of them, a Hungarian Jew, Pinchas, came up to me requesting that I give him and his two companions half of my bread rations, if not, things will go badly for me. I flatly refused to let myself be blackmailed. For not giving in to these thugs, my life was made intolerable to such a degree that I sometimes wished I would die, despite the fact that there was some little hope on the horizon: there was no sign of the SS in the barrack and rumor had it that they were fleeing gradually. We were being supervised by "our own". We were in fact in close proximity to the fighting. It seems that Jewish tradition was right. The world would be redeemed either when totally innocent, an impossible dream, or when totally guilty. The latter was an apt description of our plight. The agonizing times were drawing to a close yet the last bitter drop was still missing in our cup of tears. The cup was filled to the brim by the anguish of the Matthausen patients.

A miracle one expects can hardly be called a miracle, yet for us it did prove a veritable miracle. We knew that the Americans were nearby and we had confidence that the camp would be liberated. Despite this, not one of us had the confidence that he would survive to see it.

The Long-Awaited Miracle

On the first of May, the block elder, a Russian guard, came into our barrack with the announcement that a ceasefire had been signed. Our joy was too overwhelming for us to grasp the meaning of what was happening. True, we had waited for this moment, yet it still had caught us by surprise. Soon inmates from the other Matthausen camp came to inform us of the good news. Everything changed very quickly. The leadership of the camp tried immediately to please the inmates. While shooting was still going on, news came that the Americans were approaching and that the Red Cross would soon take over the camp. Our joy was unimaginable, yet did not cause us to forget about our stomachs. We broke open the storerooms and prepared whatever food there was.

On the sixth and seventh of May, the Americans arrived. We almost went out of our minds. Only then did we feel secure and free. Some of us still harbored a doubt whether we could count ourselves liberated. Our fear was not completely misplaced. In some camps the SS had fled, but returned several days later recapturing the camp, slaying many survivors in the process. We were lying on our planks as two American soldiers came in, armed with cameras, followed by other servicemen. We considered ourselves saved. But one could not hurry towards happiness. Happiness was still far away; for many of us it never came. The reason was a simple one. The Americans were separated from their base and had nothing to offer us other than pea-soup. The little honey, which they had taken away from the Germans, was a drop in the ocean. The huge quantity of soup, which the hungry people drank, caused dysentery. The Americans simply did not understand that you couldn't give emaciated people — corpses almost — soup; that all they could digest was crackers and tea. Instead they were cooking pea soups five or six times a day and were serving us generously.

The victims also didn't look after themselves. Our stomachs were too weak, our intestines shrunken by permanent hunger and the peas inflated us. It is difficult for me to express the tragedy of the newly liberated. The mortality rate was exceedingly high; every second person was very ill and close to death. Everyone was sick.

I also lay in terrible pain. Dr. Rotbalsam, with whom I had the doubtful good fortune of always sharing camps, had already pronounced me dead. My death would have been convenient for him, as he would have had one less witness to his deeds that would disqualify him not only as a doctor but as a human being. He, of course, offered no treatment. The Americans finally realized the situation, but for many, help came too late. Also for me the end would have been tragic, thanks to Dr. Rotbalsam. The camp was being liquidated; everything was in chaos. Other than Dr. Rotbalsam no one knew about our barrack and its sick inmates. He told no one and gave us no medical attention. By a stroke of luck, the Americans walked into our barrack, transported us, and administered blood transfusions that revitalized us a little. I was given six consecutive blood transfusions, immediately improving my condition.

Our joy was, nevertheless, marred by the fact that, despite all human efforts, many people died after liberation. The Americans showed a great deal of selflessness, they worked day and night. We were living temporarily in tents, and when on one occasion a storm broke out and threatened to blow away the tents, the American soldiers literally held up the tents with their hands. I now had time to reflect upon my situation while lying in one of those sick beds. On the one hand, the awareness that my close ones were all dead affected me deeply and I repeated Kaddish for them and wept bitterly. On the other hand, I imagined that the world must have improved and that all doors would be open to us. Unfortunately, none of this eventuated. The world had changed but little.

**Israel Jacob (Richard) Mittelberg.
Melbourne Australia 1972**

Israel Jacob (Richard) Mittelberg, Treblinka 1945, far right

Israel Jacob (Richard) Mittelberg, Treblinka 1945, third from right

Building containing deli business and apartment where Mittelberg Family
lived before the Warsaw Ghetto

David outside his late father's shop and first floor apartment in Warsaw, 54A Wspolna St. Original shop and building, Warsaw 1993

Perimeter fence of Majdanek reflecting vast size of camp

Block 22 Majdanek, dormitory where my father slept

David Mittelberg outside father's dormitory at Majdanek

Esti Mittelberg, grandaughter, reading from Hebrew translation of her grandfather's memoirs, at Majdanek, to her school delegation in 2001

Majdanek shower room for disinfection

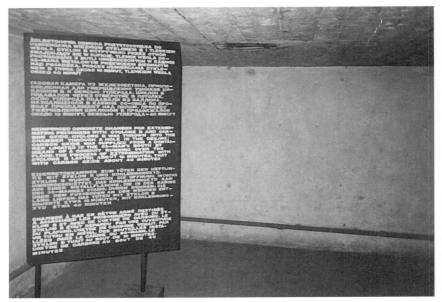

Gas Chamber, Majdanek Concentration Camp

Shoe Memorial at Majdanek Concentration Camp

Crematorium Majdanek

Block 19 Infirmary at Majdanek

Lena (Leah) Mittelberg, mother of David Mittelberg and Rachel Caplan (nee Mittelberg), Israel 2004

Mittelberg Family, Kibbutz Yizreel 2004. L–R Back Row: Yoel, David. Front Row: Esti, Shuli & Shoshana

Caplan Family, Melbourne, Australia 2004. Back: Rachel & Murray. Front: Liora & Tali

PART II

The Testament

by
David Mittelberg

A s a sociologist, I have been vitally interested in the impact of the Holocaust — both because of my own family history and because of my concern for the survival of the Jewish people. The predominantly psychological and psychiatric professional litera-

Impact of the Holocaust on Second Generation of Survivors

ture deals with the effects of the Holocaust on the second generation. These professionals coined the term "Holocaust survivor," styled the language and described the parameters of the phenomena. The writings of some of the prominent members of the second generation who discovered the meaning of this phenomenon in their own terms and in their own lives are also important. I will summarize my own research, conducted between 1978 and 1986, which sheds light on some important aspects raised in the literature.

The general portrait that arises from the clinical literature is a view of the survivor as a traumatized individual, hampering the natural/normal growth of his offspring. The trauma becomes both mutated and transmitted transgenerationally, emotionally crippling the second-generation. However criticism from within the discipline of Psychology has already correctly faulted the tendency to generalize from work with clinical groups, to the Holocaust survivor offspring at large. In addition, these reports failed to distinguish between different types of Holocaust experiences, for example concentration camps or partisan activity, nor did they examine the role that contemporary life situations play on the development of second-generation members.

An additional variable offered by scholars related to whether the survivors themselves talked about their Holocaust experience to their offspring. The argument presented is quite simple. Concentration camp survivors talked less about their experiences than did partisans, and it was the silence which was burdensome to the second generation. Mothers were found to talk more than fathers while daughters were more affected by the parents' experiences than sons. Throughout, there remains one important unanswered question, namely, is the silence, the deleterious effects of which are universally recognized, a function of the Holocaust experience itself or of the post-Holocaust environment in which the offspring were being brought up?

I cannot offer conclusive evidence to contradict the causal hypothesis referred to above, but I do wish to offer an alternative plausible hypothesis, the support for which I draw from my own biography. In Israel the Holocaust commemoration is called "The Day of the Holocaust and of Heroism". To the best of my knowledge, in the first two decades after the war, this commemoration did not bear this name anywhere else in the world — I refer, of course, to the addition of the word 'Heroism'. It would seem to me that the culture of remembering generated by the state memorials served both to legitimate the heroism (and of course, why not?), but also to de-legitimize or at least neutralize the status of survival from the concentration camps. Hence, the roar of silence, the consequent repression that follows and the need to break that silence which was superbly shown in the documentary made by Eva

Fogelman in the United States titled "Breaking the Silence".

The Jewish community in Melbourne was more than doubled, from 9,500 in 1933 to 24,000 in 1954, by Holocaust survivors, many from the concentration camps. I grew up both in a family and a community of survivors of the worst concentration camp experiences, where it was legitimate and prevalent to talk about these experiences. In addition to the formal community memorials which were just that, a collective mourning — with no illusions — survivor families often met, paradigmatically at the Passover Seder table, but in fact all year round, where they talked almost competitively and compulsively of their suffering and ordeals. It appears to me that the Jewish community in Melbourne itself served as the cathartic agent that elsewhere may have required professional and group attention.

Thus, while I agree that it is the talking about the Holocaust experience, both public and private which attenuates the effect it has on the offspring, it is by no means clear to me that this is exclusively a consequence of the particular survivor's experience itself, but crucially how this experience is mediated by the post war society itself in which the survivor and his family lives.

Among children of Holocaust survivors studied, I found that there were no indicators of parent-child alienation in comparison to their peers. Children of Holocaust survivors scored higher on indicators of Jewish identity, in positive terms, in identification with Israel and commitment to the State of Israel, and in rejection of intermarriage. The children of Holocaust survivors expressed more personal ambition for executive positions and economic independence and success. The evidence seems to suggest that even such disparate groups of young Jews as college students in Boston, kibbutz-born émigrés in America, American immigrants to Israel, artists, intellectuals, poets and lawyers, from Israel, America, Australia — the world over, share a common burden which in many cases generates a powerful commitment to the meaning of their collective past and to the importance of the collective future of the culture to which they belong.

C learly this will be a personal account, not representing all children of survivors, nor even all those who grew up in Melbourne, Australia, but I have no doubt that many will find common identification with this account. First, I wish to relate to the nature and

The New World: Reflections on Being a Child of Holocaust Survivors

structure of a family of survivors, then to the content of its educational program, and finally, I will relate to the particular outcomes that these had in my childhood and adolescence.

I was eighteen months old when my parents arrived in Australia to start a new life.

Before the war, my father owned an established wholesale and retail food business in Warsaw, while my mother worked as an accountant.

Leah (Lena) Mittelberg nee Marmelstein actually knew my father before the war as she was an assistant accountant to her father, my grandfather Pinchas Marmelstein, in my father's business. In 1939 she left Warsaw for Kremenic with her brother Hersh and his wife Pola, to live with their parents. With Hitler's increasing rise to power, they ran away from Kremenic in 1941, fled deep into Russia and stayed there until 1945. My mother returned to Poland after the war. There she met up with my father in Lodz, where they later married in 1946.

On arrival in Australia, they took the only option open to them and opened a stall in the Victoria Market. After a few years of success, they expanded their business by buying a garment shop in a fashionable suburb where my mother worked long days all week. Both businesses were maintained simultaneously until my parents made Aliya to Israel.

Many families of survivors consisted of small nuclear "new immigrant" families. The parents were far older than non- survivor parents with a large age gap between parents and children. The children grew up without grandparents and very often without uncles or aunts. My own family was marked by an overriding concern for economic survival and reconstruction, with the emphasis on achievement and success, both of the parents and the children. My parents felt their success increased through the achievements of my sister Rachel, and me. While all this applied to my family, my mother, my father, my sister and me, these were not the only parameters of our family life. Not only survival, but Jewish survival, Jewish commitment, Jewish involvement were hallmarks of our conversations and our activities.

There were tensions between the different claims that these goals would place on our time and on our minds. We were a Zionist family and the Hebraic activists of Zionism looked askance on the Yiddish language. In spite of this, my sister and I attended a Yiddish kindergarten; Yiddish was our mother tongue. Yet our family was a Zionist family and our father never ceased to speak about Israel and his goal to go there. All the economic hardships notwithstanding, my father was a community activist from the outset. He was a founder and Vice President of the Association of Former Concentration Camp Inmates in Melbourne, was a delegate to the Jewish Community council of Victoria (formerly the Victorian Jewish Board of Deputies), active in the United Israel Appeal, the Kadimah Yiddish theatre and cultural activities, Jewish Welfare (Hilfsfund), Poale Zion, the Montefiore Homes for the Aged, and so on. My mother was similarly active in WIZO and other service organizations. Finally, prior to my freshman year in college in 1964, my father went alone on a pilgrimage to Israel. "I do not want to leave this world without setting foot in the Land of Israel," he said and achieved his desire, despite his Holocaust induced heart disease, the expense, and the necessity to leave my mother alone with us to manage the businesses while he was away.

At the age of six, my parents took me out of the Yiddish kinder-garten and placed me in the local elementary school in a pre-dominantly Jewish neighborhood. School hours were from a quarter to nine until a quarter to four. I then continued studying

A Jewish Education

from 4:10 P.M. in the afternoon until 6:30 P.M. every day at the cheder or Talmud Torah five days a week. On Sundays I attended Talmud Torah from 9:00 A.M. until 1:00 P.M. Here already the tensions began: the public school was a mixture of Jews and non-Jews, and the Talmud Torah was an orthodox religious establishment, which assumed Orthodox rit-ual practices both in the institution and at home. The Talmud Torah required synagogue attendance on Shabbat. My father wished to provide basic religious training for me; he himself was not a strict observer of Shabbat. "We must survive, my son," he explained. "So, we must work on Shabbat," he added as we pre-pared a load of clothing to bring to our market stall at 5:30 A.M. on Saturday morning. At the same time, the richness of the cycle of the Jewish year filled our home: we were a traditional Jewish fam-ily, with a festive Friday night meal and celebration of the High Holy Days, Passover, and Chanukah.

My parents were in the shmatte (rag trade) business, selling women's garments in the Victoria Market where many Holocaust survivors began their economic recovery in Melbourne, Australia. They were successful at it also, and Saturday was the best day in the business. Even in the years prior to my Bar Mitzvah, at the apex of my religious training, I would finish my school attendance on a Friday at 3:30 P.M. and run to the market to help my ill father pack up the stall. Angina Pectoris was only one of his chronic afflictions. We had to set up, take down and pack up the stall every day at the market; there were no permanent booths at all. We would return home sometimes after the Shabbat; in winter this was almost always the case. After helping my father set up, I would run home before 8:00 A.M., shower, dress in Shabbat clothes, go to the Synagogue, fulfill my obligations to the Talmud Torah and come home again after the *kiddush,* change my clothes and return to the market to help my father. There was no choice; these obligations had to be carried out.

In my earlier memories, I remember the tensions between our Yiddish-speaking friends: Bundist non-Zionists as well as anti-Zionists or communists and our friends who were religious, orthodox and non-secular. All these tensions I carried with me as part of being a Jew. Troubled by these contradictions I asked, "Dad, everyone thinks they have the right way — who is right?" He answered, "You should learn everything: when you are old enough to decide you will decide; first of all you have to know." My Jewish education was a direct consequence of his intensely expressed commitment to Jewish survival — his and mine.

When I was growing up in Australia, school was compulsory only until the 8th grade. Family solidarity and support were primary values for the Italian and Greek immigrant families of our neighborhood — as well as for the Jewish families. I had a friend who started selling newspapers in 6th grade and dropped out of school in 8th grade to work full time to help his family. I was feeling so much pressure from my hectic schedule. One day, when I was in 8th grade I asked, "Dad, what about me quitting school so I can help you more?" He thought for a moment and then said emphatically, "No, no. You must continue to study and to share in the burden of family economic survival." But finally I was caught. Someone reported me working on Shabbat to the Rabbi and others at the Talmud Torah. "How can you break Shabbes and you are almost a Bar Mitzvah?" scolded the Rabbi and congregants. At a meeting with the Rabbi my father stated, "I have a bad heart, thanks to the Holocaust and must have David's help to keep the business going." I continued in Talmud Torah and continued to help my father. Some of the other guys quit the Talmud Torah after Bar Mitzvah. The teachers captured my interest with the new and fascinating world of Talmud study and I continued studying for another year and a half.

Many of my school friends were also second generation of Holocaust survivors. During my elementary and high school years many friends lost their parents, who were the same age as my parents — a delayed effect of the Holocaust itself. Indeed when we used to read the "Australian Jewish News," the Jewish communal newspaper on Friday nights; like everybody else we looked first at the back pages to see not sports news — of little interest — but the death announcements: to learn who had lost a father or a mother or a friend this week. Funerals and funeral services were something that we were quite used to. Some of our close friends had come to Australia before the war. My sister Rachel and I were often envious of them for their more natural seeming home environment, including outdoor fun and a tension-free existence. As children we could not articulate the difference: extra responsibilities to our parents.

The contradictory demands of religious Jewish and Zionist consciousness and action inevitably led me into the domain of Zionist activism and thus, with my father's encouragement, I at the age of nine became a member of Habonim, the Labor Zionist Youth Movement, instead of the Orthodox Bnei Akiva. I eventually became a youth leader, with ever more responsibilities. Many years later in Israel, I called this the Akkedat Avraham phenomenon — a recurrent theme in my life. Akkedat Yitzchak refers to the willingness of Abraham to sacrifice his son Issac in accordance with the will of God and as a sign of supreme and divine commitment. In my terms Akkedat Avraham means: should a son sacrifice his only father, in order to realize goals or fulfill ideological or value commitments?

Thus my involvement in camps and other activities was always in tension with my responsibilities to my parents, and most of all to my father, since most of the movement's activities were on Friday, Saturday, or Sunday and the peak work period was on Friday and Saturday. So many responsibilities had to be fulfilled in such a short time and each in contradiction with the other. These responsibilities were shared equally with my sister Rachel, however the question reached its peak in 1965 when I was offered a scholarship to go to Israel for a year — to attend the Institute for Youth Leaders from Abroad. My parents and I agonized over this most difficult decision. They agreed that I should go to Israel for that year and I went, hoping and wondering whether my father would survive the year until I came home.

As a teenager, driving to Habonim meetings, I regularly dropped my father off at the Montefiore Old Age Home. "How can you stay with those old people for hours?" I asked. At that age I could not understand how my father could take the precious time from his busy work schedule and community responsibilities. "They are lonely and enjoy talking to a fellow Jew in Yiddish," he answered. "And unfortunately," he added, "many of their children are too busy to visit very much." When I went to pick him up I could see the eyes of the residents, glowing with the happiness of being treated with kindness and respect by my father. And now it is my turn: my mother is in a seniors' home, twenty minutes from our kibbutz, and my wife Shoshana and I visit her five times a week, while my sister Rachel calls her almost every day from Australia.

It goes without saying, of course, that Holocaust Remembrance and, more specifically, the Warsaw Ghetto commemoration played a very important part in our family calendar. My parents came from Warsaw and my father survived the Warsaw Ghetto. On many occasions, I or my sister served as community symbols, lighting memorial candles at the cemetery memorial or in other communal functions which we attended every year as a family. We did not commemorate the Holocaust only then. The Pesach Seder in our family always began with a one-minute silence commemorating the Nazi invasion of the Ghetto on the eve of Pesach 1943. The liberation of the Jews from Egyptian bondage was linked inextricably with the survival of contemporary Jews from Nazi bondage. To this day, every year when I conduct the Seder in my own home I continue this silent commemoration with my children and I hope they will continue to do so with their children.

The year in Israel was critical in redefining the values of my Jewish commitment. I had long since left the Talmud Torah and had gone through a stage of rejection of traditional Orthodoxy; it seemed outdated, archaic. It was not yet clear to me how being in Israel and being Jewish would come together,

The Israel Experience and Its Consequences

but during that year I learned Hebrew and basically relearned what it meant to be Jewish; how one could be both modern and Jewish at the same time. At that point, I think I probably decided that in one form or another I would resolve these tensions in Israel and in kibbutz: the tensions between the religious and the secular, between Israel and the Diaspora, between the particular and the universal, between Yiddish and Hebrew.

I returned to Australia, taking on a senior role in Habonim, and I developed a public profile as a Zionist activist in the Jewish community and as a radical activist in the campus community. And yet another tension arose in 1967, when I was enrolled in Monash University, at that time the center of student radicalism in Australia and well-linked with student radicalism around the world — at least through the media. I again wore two hats: I was a universalist left-

wing radical and a committed Zionist activist. The tensions and
the contradictions reached their peak in both an emotional and
ideological level in the events that preceded the Six-Day-War. The
historical background to the Six-Day-War and the atmosphere both
in Israel and the Diaspora needs no documentation here.
Testimony from Israeli soldiers, as found in the book *Seventh Day*,
as well as in much other material in the Israeli press reflect the
feeling that the future collective survival of the Jewish people in
general and Israel in particular were being threatened once again.
No one actually spoke the words 'potential Holocaust', but we all
wondered: will the Jewish people survive? My background com-
pelled me as well as many friends to volunteer for Israel.
Enrollment required parental permission, so I approached my
mother, not my father, to sign the papers. She signed.

The war — mercifully — ended quickly and I did not get called
by the volunteer board. I found out later that my father had asked
the local Israel representative, behind my back, to register me on
a lower priority because he was unable to spare me . Very few
seats were available on flights to Israel, so the representative com-
plied and later said to me, "Taking care of the Zionist youth movement is just as important as being in Israel after the war." I did not
quite agree with him at the time.

The period prior to the Six-Day-War provided a special and
unanticipated test for me. Nasser, leader of the Arab, world threatened Israel. My response as a Zionist activist: demonstrations,
marches, and protests. On the evening of May 24, 1967 I convened
and chaired a meeting of the leadership of the Zionist youth movements where we decided to organize a youth march through the
streets of Melbourne with posters and placards, joining the whole
Jewish community in a rally in support of Israel at the Sydney
Myer Music Bowl. On the 25th of May, the Board of Management
of the Executive Council of Australian Jewry applied massive pres-

sure on us to cancel the march.

That same evening, the State Zionist Council of Victoria met and debated the request of the ECAJ who had agreed to support the Zionist rally at the Sydney Myer Music Bowl to be held on Sunday afternoon on May 28, but had decided to oppose the Youth March. This was debated at the Council and, in the final analysis, the March was approved. In the few days between Wednesday and the following Sunday, I was personally placed under a great deal of pressure to call off the March by the senior and prominent leadership of the Australian Jewish Community who, I suppose, were genuinely concerned and convinced that this 'radical' strategy would harm Israel as well as the Jewish community in Australia.

"David, would you risk the support for Israel's cause by the international community and the Australian Government in the United Nations, through a hurried, reckless measure such as a demonstration?" the senior Jewish leaders asked forcefully. Their position, of course, reflected their conservative politics, which I did not share. But their arguments caused me a great deal of concern and, once again, I found myself having to choose between contradictory goals, between organized Jewish leadership and between my own understanding of what that leadership should be doing and my own values. Despite the limited advance publicity the March had received, a massive demonstration assembled under the supervision of the Victoria Police, with their protection and their authorization. Senior representatives of the Executive Council of Australian Jewry arrived and pleaded, "Call the demonstration off before it's too late." I responded, "That is no longer possible." The March turned out to be a big success; I think the senior leadership also was both relieved and pleased.

Exactly a year later I was in Israel as a youth delegate to the 27th World Zionist Congress and I related the story to my Israeli friends. They said, "We heard on that Sunday that there were demonstrations in Melbourne, London and New York, and we knew that you were there." I felt a glow of accomplishment. I had not been able to fly to Israel in her hour of need, but had accomplished something of importance for Israel — yes, I had been there. But I was not only there with my friends and relatives in Israel: I was there with people who had not yet become my friends, but were to become so for the rest of my life.

The year 1968 was exciting in the world of youth politics. The World Zionist Congress in 1968 was very exciting also, and the youth delegates at the Congress were part of that movement of youth politics and proud of it. It was heady for Jews who were experiencing the euphoric relief from the threat of destruction and the joy of the reunification of Jerusalem. How different that period looks now. For many of us it was an opportunity to reconcile and integrate our radical interests, our universalistic concerns, and our collectivist commitment to Jewish identity, continuity and sovereignty. In those days "National Self Determination" was the catch phrase around which revolutions were made and legitimacy was based, and we grabbed with two hands that legitimization of our Jewish modernity, our socialism and our Zionism. At that Congress, I met young people my age, many of whom were children of Holocaust survivors (although I did not for a moment use that term at that time), from Montreal, Berkeley, New York, London and Paris. We shared our common, radical Zionist experiences on campus. I remember riding in a bus with a friend who had escaped from Dubczek-ruled Czechoslovakia. My friend was filled with optimism; to this day I have no idea what happened to him.

At the Congress itself I was elected to the executive of the youth delegation and was heavily involved in politicking at that time, working towards elections for what we thought would be a revolution in the leadership of the Zionist movements. What was more important, though, was the networking that we all did with each other in the youth delegation which served us on our return to our home societies in many different ways, primarily as an information network. We exchanged with each other articles that we wrote — the responsa we wrote in the campus newspapers which we edited, defending Israel and the Jewish people from its enemies on the left and on the right and from its 'so called' friends in the center. We shared communality of time and of culture, although not of space. This collectivity and the common fate of the Peoplehood that we shared were clear to me without question. Our shared dedication to Israel was transcendentally meaningful above and beyond the meaning of the comfortable and relatively problem-free everyday life that I continued to lead in Australia.

On my return from the Congress, I continued to work in the youth movement, serving as general secretary of Habonim. I continued to complete my honors degree in sociology and politics while continuing as a political activist at Monash University, involved in student government. I also helped to establish the radical Zionist movement at Monash, was involved in national student politics, national Jewish student politics, and in the Jewish community addressing the community on a number of different occasions including, finally, the community-wide annual commemoration of the Warsaw Ghetto uprising, held in 1970 at the Melbourne Town Hall.

The youth delegation had successfully called for democratization of the Zionist Movement at the 1968 Congress. In my final year in Australia, in which I taught Politics at Monash University and Sociology at the Royal Melbourne Institute of Technology, it was indeed resolved to conduct Zionist elections the world over, including Australia. Thus prior to my Aliyah to Israel, I ran as a candidate for that Congress on behalf of the Labor Zionists in the national elections. Subsequently, the Labor Zionist ticket which I

110

headed was able to send one mandate to the Zionist Congress. My participation in the World Zionist Congress in 1972 as a delegate was my last act as a representative of the Australian Jewish community and my first act as a citizen in Israeli politics.

I referred earlier to Akkedat Avraham, a theme which was part of my life on three separate occasions. The first was in my Zionist activism, often conflicting with my commitments to my parents; the second was the actual act of Aliyah, also conflicting with my responsibilities to my parents. In fact, prior to my Aliyah I actually liquidated my father's businesses so that he would not need to work after my departure

Aliya and Akkeda

from Australia. But the third component of Akkedat Avraham did not impact my own parents, but the parents of my partner for life. My wife Shoshana is the only daughter of the late Rabbi Jacob and Esther Kotlar of Perth in Australia. The Kotlars were also from Europe, also Holocaust survivors, who had migrated to Palestine immediately after the War. Shoshana was born in Israel after a number of miscarriages and was the one and only child who could be born. The Kotlars had lived in Israel for five years after walking across Europe, a Europe in which they lost all their families. They had endured the War of Independence, following which they came to Australia for a year or two on *shlichut* (as emissaries). Rabbi Kotlar was employed as a *shochet* (a ritual slaughterer) for the isolated Perth Jewish Community. Rabbi Kotlar, an ordained Orthodox Rabbi from Kletzk Yeshiva in Lithuania, faithfully served the Perth Jewish Community as Rabbi, Shochet, *Chazan* (cantor), and Dayan (judge), for nearly forty years. Up to the day we came on Aliyah, Shoshana had never visited Israel nor had her parents. In a large part this reflected the fact that throughout the entire forty years Rabbi Kotlar did not take a single vacation to anywhere, lest the community be left without kosher meat. On the other hand, this long absence from Israel was really strange considering that Shoshana's late mother was a powerful personality with a very powerful political profile. An intensely religious person of very high intellect, she had been educated in a Hebrew day school in Europe near Bialystock, had belonged to the Zionist pioneering youth group *Hechalutz,* had been a member of the political party *Mapai* and a delegate to the national convention of *Mapai* in Israel and knew personally most of the leading figures at that time in Israel. For her, I suspect, the departure to Australia was a functional necessity but an ideological disaster.

Shoshana and I met in January 1969 in Melbourne at a demonstration which I helped organize to protest the tragic and barbaric hanging of nine Iraqi Jews. As fate would have it, Shoshana, visiting Melbourne, had clearly attended that demonstration as part of her Jewish commitment, meeting me by chance through common friends; the rest is history. To have taken Shoshana, an only daughter, from her Orthodox religious parents, who had lived in Israel out of Zionist commitment but had left, and to wrench her away to Israel and to a secular kibbutz was for me once again, *Akkedat Avraham.* The power, perhaps the chutzpa to do that, the ability to cope with the tensions that that situation generated, I have no doubt arose from the powerful commitment that I felt to the Jewish people and to the necessity that Aliyah was for the Jewish People, which needed to transcend even responsibility to parents: my own and Shoshana's.

Shoshana and I shared much in common. Our parents were Holocaust survivors. We were both Yiddish speakers. We were both children of parents who had lost most of their families. We had both lived in incomplete environments. Perth was a vibrant community. Yet Shoshana was a member of one of the few orthodox families in that vibrant community. Paradoxically perhaps, those different forms of incompleteness set the stage for the search together for an alternative contemporary Jewish way of life. Currently, we live on a secular Israeli kibbutz, Yizreel. Shoshana is a software engineer with Maytronics, Inc. And yet, traditional Jewish observance is part of our life.

My sister Rachel lives in Melbourne, married to Murray Caplan, whose parents were pre-war migrants from Poland. They have two daughters, Tali and Liora. Rachel recently retired after eighteen years as Executive Director of the State Zionist Council of Victoria and was given the Chaim Weizman Award in recognition of her dedicated service to the Zionist movement. Rachel, who continues to be active as a lay leader in WIZO and the Jewish Agency's Partnership 2000 in Australia, visits us once a year, to spend time with our family, as well as participating in Zionist conferences.

Life in Israel: Politics and Research

Life on kibbutz presented new and different problems and tensions. Apart from the biographical questions of individual survival we had to face the question: what is an Israeli Jewish identity? Similarly, the question of what is the Jewish character of kibbutz life raises itself and has yet to be resolved for us. Over the years, there have been different attempts to relate to these questions. I grappled, myself, with different approaches to Jewish ritual and tradition in the kibbutz and outside of it.

In the years 1979 and 1980 I was drafted to be the World General Secretary of Habonim and, once again, returned to public political or Zionist political life. Once again I left the comfortable everyday world of the kibbutznik, for the more public profile, which was concerned with the Jewish identity of young Jews primarily those who had not yet come to Israel. Those were heady years as well in which I had my first insight into the nature of

Israeli politics, in the Kibbutz Movement and the larger Israeli society, primarily through the intensive relationship that I developed with the late Mussa Harif, then General Secretary of the *Ichud Hakvutzot ve'Kibbutzim* Federation, and later to be a young and short-lived member of Knesset. When Mussa was tragically killed in a car accident, it was clear to me that if the political venue were an option for searching out the meaning of Jewish collective survival in Israel, it was one not to be adopted by me in the coming decades.

To this point I have said much about Holocaust survivors and children of Holocaust survivors, yet the term itself did not come to my own attention until 1981, ten years after my Aliyah to Israel, and after many more years of Zionist and political activism. This occurred when I read in the Israeli press about a forthcoming First World Conference of Holocaust survivors and within that, a conference for second generation of Holocaust survivors. I was told about Helen Epstein's book *Children of the Holocaust* (1980), which I read with much interest and some suspicion. After lengthy inquiry, I made contact with the organizers and, ultimately, was invited to lead a workshop on the social and political implications of the Holocaust for the second generation of survivors.

I want to record here two strong impressions from that conference (I have since had the opportunity, years later, of checking and reconfirming with other participants, especially from the Diaspora, that these feelings were commonly shared by others as well). The first, which I cannot document scientifically, was a powerful feeling of commonality and commitment. The people who were there, hundreds of young people, were all my age; we looked similar, we spoke alike, even though we were from all the four corners of the world. Some did not have a high Jewish profile and it did not matter whether they were from secular or religious backgrounds, with kippot or without. Many had been to Israel before, participating in a variety of programs and many were articulate and articulately concerned with their own Jewishness and with Jewish collective survival. I felt in the room a vibrant energy and a deep identification of Jewish men and women with each other, a sharing which I felt could — ought — to be powerful, positive, creative and innovative.

But, together with this feeling, there was my second impression which was of massive disappointment — an alienation, a lack of communication, a dissonance. This occurred in the plenum of the second generation, during an address by an Israeli who made a well intentioned but very unsuccessful plea for the immediate Aliyah of all the participants, implying that their failure to do so was a rejection of their historic responsibilities. The speaker was a Sabra and the audience was, in large part, from the Diaspora. I felt a gap between the speaker and the audience all around me; I felt hostility rising and I wanted to say to the speaker, "Oh God, you are losing them; this is no way to develop an Israel-Diaspora dialogue." The speaker had no idea of what was happening.

I had to leave the conference early to take care of my two young children on the kibbutz. My wife Shoshana and I had both been registered for it (we do not usually go to the same conferences), but just a few days prior to the conference, Shoshana's mother passed away in Australia and she flew home for the funeral. I left hurriedly without saying goodbye and without getting to know the other participants. This was a meeting as important as the 1968 congress, since here I met some of the leaders of the second generation network, several of whom I actually only got to know later through the common memory we had of that conference. Principal among them were Eva Fogelman and Menachem Rosensaft.

It was only from this time that I myself began to articulate the notion of a particular consciousness of a second generation of

Holocaust survivors. I don't think this was by chance, since we members of the second generation were becoming adults and bringing up our own children. We were asking ourselves the same questions of Jewish continuity and survival, although now in an adult frame and directed to our children, more so than to ourselves. We asked not the questions of what have we become but rather of what will our children be and what will their future be, what will be the future of the Jewish people, the matrix of our children's future lives?

For me, the next relevant event was my participation in a symposium at the Diaspora Museum, chaired by the late Dr. Shamai Davidson, the distinguished psychiatrist and scholar of the Second Generation phenomena. Eva Fogelman showed her excellent movie, entitled "Breaking the Silence." I was in a panel discussing the movie. It was clear that the movie was based on at least two things: (1) "Breaking the Silence" referred to Holocaust survivors who did not talk about their past to their children; their children discovered the family history either in late adolescence or early adulthood and (2) the need for that sort of activity in a therapeutic environment. I, of course, knew that many Holocaust survivors did speak of their experiences with their children; they talked about them privately and they talked about them in a communal atmosphere. However, whether they did or did not do so was perhaps related to the community in which they lived.

I also knew that until that point in time, I had not come across anybody in my generation who had engaged in therapy as a consequence of being the son or daughter of Holocaust survivors, but I had met many friends, who had one or another form of ideological commitment — whether to a secular radical cause or a Bundist Jewish cause or a Zionist secular or Zionist religious cause, or just ordinary — if you like — Jewish commitment expressed in Jewish community leadership. These were the responses with which

I was acquainted, which while clearly not the only responses, could not be ignored in any typology of second generation responses to the Holocaust. Elsewhere (Mittelberg, 1989), I have made a formal attempt at spinning out the dimensions that such a typology might form.

What remained for me, however, from the 1981 gathering of Holocaust survivors was the commitment to an Israel-Diaspora dialogue, the search for a language of discovery and communication between Jews the world over. As an Israeli now, it seemed I had absolutely no way to further that goal. Israeli society appeared and still appears as sectarian and divisive, unable to generate national leadership or to clearly define contemporary Zionist goals. Israeli society is over-dominated by party politics and is lacking in national consensus, unable to engage, it would seem, in a meaningful dialogue with world Jewry of my generation.

The opportunity to be involved in Israeli-Diaspora dialogue arose for me with the establishment of the Israel Forum. Once again, fate played its role, and by word of mouth I was invited to attend the founding meeting of the Israel Forum. I eventually took an important (for me) role, primarily through its dominant activity which had been basically the motif of my life to this point, namely, the bringing of Jewish youth to Israel.

The Israel Forum, is a non-partisan coalition of Israelis from all walks of life whose mandate was Israeli-Diaspora dialogue. I joined the lay committee that would conceive and then implement Project Otzma. I felt it to be the natural place in which I could contribute what little knowledge I had to that activity. After a year, Otzma was born, a program in which volunteers from North America spend a year in Israel, and it continues to grow. I have since been elected to the executive of the Israel Forum and been very active in its Israel-Diaspora dialogue as well as in the lay leadership of the Otzma program. It is an exciting experience, an arena and a process at the same time. I felt for the first time that my Israeli commitment to being Jewish and my Jewish commitment to being Israeli were beginning to coalesce in a statement of purpose and a purpose of action. I am not at all sure what the final outcome of the Forum activities will be. It has voluntarism as its keynote activity, and Israel-Diaspora relations as its mandate, which is another way of saying dealing with the continuity of the Jewish people and the future character of the Jewish people.

Dealing with the Israel-Diaspora dimension on a non-partisan basis, Otzma must necessarily avoid many controversial issues, otherwise its uniqueness will be quickly destroyed. This is both a strength and an inherent weakness. It thus avoids, for the time being at least, yet another burning tension which I feel today and which I think many Israelis feel. This is the tension between the commitment to Jewish identity and the Jewish collective on the one hand and to the democratic way of life in Israel on the other. It will be recalled that for me, Aliyah to Israel was to have resolved all of those conflicts, and here in 1988 it appeared that one had to begin all over again. The relationship between the democracy of Israel and the Jewish or Zionist character of Israel appeared to be in tension; herein lies one of the major outcomes of the unholy alliance between secular Zionism and State religion.

Both were in search of a basis for contemporary legitimacy. Secular Zionists sought, quite rightly so, the Jewish basis for a revolution in a contemporary Jewish world and the religious sought the basis for the legitimacy of the Rabbinate in the contemporary state. In pre-1967 Israel the search for a basis of contemporary legitimacy was expressed in a political coalition. After 1967 that coalition was exploded by the transformation of the political options into religious options, restricting the decision making process to the question of divine intervention thereby relegating the question of compromise and democratic decision making secondary to the question of the divine will and the divine intention.

A political system cannot be regulated simultaneously on the basis of authority that is divinely inspired and on one that is democratically governed. It is a tension that Israelis have yet to work out and I fear, may have to pay a very heavy price or maybe even, God forbid, the supreme sacrifice. It is a tension that has run through the relationship between Israel and its Arab neighbors. I fear that the basis of legitimacy of the different national movements will come down to the basis of legitimacy of competing divine orders. In that state of affairs no compromise will be possible and no solution will ever be found.

Similarly, in the relationships between Israeli Jews and Jews in the Diaspora, Jews who live in a democratic world, supporting democratic rules for political life, have not been able to identify with an Israel in which the democratic regime is subservient, actually secondary, to the rules of a Messianic order. Thus, the State which was set up (and it was set up, it didn't just come about) in order to realize the goals of Jewish redemption, has been undermined — perhaps worse than that — by the transformation of Jewish redemption or redemption for the Jews by the Messianic redemption, as a political goal. As a Jew living in Israel today who shares the yearning for redemption of the Jewish people but cannot agree that that redemption should be at the expense of the universal principles of democracy or the rights of other human beings, nor feel that Israel's future can be separated from the future of the rest of the Jewish world, I fear both for the future and for the legitimacy of the future of Israel.

Therefore, when I try to formulate for myself what is my Jewishness and what will be the Jewishness of my children, what is the place of democracy as opposed to extremism in contemporary Israeli life, I cannot but relate to the survival of the Jewish people, the *collective* survival of the Jewish people, as an overriding goal, even surpassing the goal of divine redemption. In Judaism, divine redemption is not something that is to occur in the world to come, after the destruction; it is something that has to happen in this world, according to the rules of everyday life in the contemporary world. All this requires the clarification of what it is to be Jewish in Israel, and what it is to be an Israeli if you are not Jewish, and what it is to be a Jew if you are not in Israel, and how all these coexist in a world that is not Jewish in its entirety.

The Holocaust underlines the tragic precariousness of collective Jewish survival; it is a truism to say that it cannot be taken for granted. Too quickly, perhaps, the existence of the State of Israel has been taken for granted, while its Jewish and democratic character has been taken as self-evident and self-sustaining, yet both of these need to be re-envisioned in each generation, recreated and reinterpreted in accordance with the period in which we live.

In the 1970's and 80's I was engaged in two research projects. One examined how the kibbutz in particular and Israel in general impact or affect the Jewish identity and Zionist commitment of young Jews from the Diaspora who temporarily visit Israel — the "Israel Experience" as it has come to be called. At the same time, I was engaged in a research project questioning the phenomenon of young Israelis leaving Israel for the Jewish and non-Jewish world outside the sovereign state. Why is it that the burden of sovereignty is becoming increasingly less tolerable to young Jews living in Israel first of all, and to other young Jews who live in the Diaspora? Yerida (emigration) and Aliyah are two sides of the same coin, and they are not just a function of the Jewishness of this generation, but the reinterpretation of the Jewishness and the reinterpretation of the character of the Jewish collective that together determine the ultimate decision about how and in which way people identify their own individual survival with the survival of the group or the People to which they belong. Being a contemporary Jew remains a dilemma, one where the burdens of joy need to be balanced against the burdens of sadness. As I see it, a responsible Jew cannot adopt only the burdens of joy which are part of being a Jew but must also shoulder the burdens of sadness, the difficult parts of being a Jew in terms of affirmative commitment to its ethical code, and to the needs for the survival of the Jewish sovereignty — the burdens of which are the price that this sovereignty demands.

When one sets out on a journey, he carries with him, on the one hand, his previous journeys, and on the other hand, the horizons of his future. My visit to Poland was a continuation and indeed a climax to all I had experienced and done in my life, and

In Their Footsteps: Poland 1993

perhaps, will symbolize a new line of thought and action in the future. One example of this complex and interwoven connection was the chance meeting I had in the Institute of Jewish History in Warsaw with a French journalist, who had recognized my name tag, and knew my French aunt, whom I also had never met, but who had recently completed a movie entitled "The last Passover in Warsaw." Examples such as this emphasize the continuity of life. Stories I heard from my father about what he and his parents experienced, took on a more profound meaning in the reality of Warsaw.

I traveled to Poland with a Jewish international delegation — a group of volunteers from the Israel Forum and the International Jewish Forum. The delegation was very interesting. People of various ages and nationalities participated: from England, Latvia, Lithuania, Estonia, Austria, France, USA, Germany, Yugoslavia, Portugal and Israel (there was not a single representative from Russia).

The second experience was a visit to my late father's house. Most, Jews and others, come to Warsaw looking for the past, for the Ghetto. They wander the streets and search in vain for the Ghetto that has been erased. The large park where all the memorial ceremonies took place sits on the site where the crowded Ghetto had been, bearing no memorial at all. All the memories revolve around the events of the past, and not those of today. I brought back to Israel a picture of the street where my mother had grown up in Karmelicka. She shouted, "This is not my street, not at all. There is no resemblance." It was the same street, the same name, the same location, and yet, not at all the same street anymore.

I found my father's house, since it had been outside the Ghetto walls, a few streets away from the Ghetto, on the Aryan aide. Closely following the stories and the theories, I arrived at Spulna Street, number 54A, and found the building still standing, not damaged, not destroyed. My father's grocery store remains in place and still functions as a food market, as it had for over sixty years. When the Ghetto was diminished, my father had been forced to leave this store, and move into the Ghetto itself. His place of dwelling within the Ghetto was destroyed.

The building my father had lived in was an apartment block (4–5 floors), and most of its inhabitants had been Jews. My father lived in the apartment directly above his store. During my present visit, I learned that the apartment directly above the store was now a hairdressing salon. I decided to enter, in order to see the place that had been my father's. The owners of the place however, would not permit us to enter. I was not alone on my visit, and a woman who had accompanied me was of the opinion that the owner of the hairdressing salon had recognized me (people tell me that I closely resemble my father and my grandfather) and had feared that I had come to repossess the property. Apparently, the matter of repossession of property is a serious threat in Poland today, and people are quite preoccupied by their fears. Therefore, the building where my father had lived was primarily rented and not owned by its inhabitants. This was enough for the first day of my stay in Warsaw, and I decided that I would return later in my journey.

Indeed, on my last day in Poland, when I returned to the apartment block, I asked the people there whether they had known my family. No one knew a thing. Just as we were leaving the grounds of the building, there suddenly appeared a man in a hat and a black coat who answered affirmatively the question of my traveling companion, a member of the Polish Forum, that yes, he had known my family. He had not lived in this apartment block before the War, but he had lived in the neighborhood, and he used to buy cheese in my father's store. He had little to tell me except for the German expulsion of the Jews to the Ghetto. Yet the fact that this one man had been familiar with my family was very exciting. It was also exciting that I had found a real connection to my family; most of the others in the delegation had not found anything.

In the place where once stood a great synagogue of Warsaw, which was destroyed at the hands of the Nazis, stands a building containing an exhibition of the Ringlebloom Archives of the Jewish Historical Museum. It is said, that during construction of the building, the builders had run into many strange and difficult problems. The Polish builders who knew that in this place had stood a synagogue, brought ten rabbis from all over the world to "expel evil spirits" (I believe that 10 men were called to say afternoon prayers — what else was there to do there?). After the services, the building proceeded smoothly. After the building was completed, one floor was assigned in gratitude to the Jewish Historical Museum.

The Concentration Camps

The concentration camp of Treblinka is today only a memorial site. In the place nothing remains of the instruments of mass murder that took place there. The camp is located in a forest, hidden from the eye; this camp was purely an extermination camp, nothing else was done here. It is said that in Treblinka **Treblinka** 2,000 people were exterminated every fifty minutes. The Treblinka of today is a site of stones. Each stone marks a community. Treblinka was closed towards the end of the War because there were no more Jews in the area. The Nazis were therefore able to destroy the camp before the end of the War.

When the Warsaw Ghetto was liquidated in 1943, and the Jews were transferred to Treblinka, those Jews who were part of a passive civil resistance, living in bunkers throughout the war, did not give themselves up until the Nazis went through the Ghetto, searching bunker by bunker, and caught them. This group numbered around 10,000 people, including members of my family.

Upon arrival at Treblinka, a selection took place. Five hundred and seven people remained on the station platform; all the rest of the group were sent to be exterminated (among these the twelve year old son of my father and the boy's mother). Those who remained on the platform knew that they were parting from their families forever, and decided to say Kaddish together as they were leaving by train. My father was among those few selected to remain on the platform, mainly due to his appearance: he wore a heavy winter coat due to the extreme physical conditions he was in. He also had a ruddy face, which gave the impression of health, although he was already thirty eight. The survivors of the action left for a journey which continued for two years, from concentration camp to concentration camp, with the knowledge that they had lost their entire families.

We also continued our journey to the rest of the concentration camps. The concentration camps of Auschwitz and Birkenau are located near the city of Crakow, in southern Poland. The Treblinka camp is near Warsaw, and the Maidanek camp is near Lublin. On our way to Crakow, we viewed the Polish countryside through the window, the Poland that looks like the Middle Ages. In Warsaw, a number of new buildings have been built over ruins. The rest of Poland looks as if it has stood still in time for the last five hundred years. The main agricultural tools of the agrarian farmer are the horse and wagon, just as they appear in old films. Poland is a pastoral land with large forests, flat, vast, unchanging, with a population of very simple people, both in dress and in work. It appeared to me from the bus that 70-80% of the farmers still cultivate with a horse and plough reattached each time to the wagon; I saw peasants sowing entirely by hand.

Upon arriving at Auschwitz, one sees sparkling red brick buildings, row after row of buildings, with barbed wire fences around them. It all looks very permanent. The infamous entrance with the sign "Work Makes Free;" it was mainly a work camp.

Auschwitz There were in this camp a few crematoria and gas chambers, however, it served principally as a work camp with many tortures. The Germans, in their compulsion to organize and be precise, made sure to set up large fields where the inmates could be counted throughout each day, wide open to bitter cold and wind. All survivors recount such torturous inspections, conducted hour after hour. For the German soldier, it must be mentioned that huts were put up, in order that they not tire. Such order and precision as evidenced in the whole site was difficult for the mind to absorb. The camp of Birkenau is larger in area than that of Auschwitz, containing a great many crematoria and large wooden huts. The murder that took place there was on a much larger scale. In both Birkenau and in Auschwitz we said Kaddish for a member of our delegation from England whose parents had perished there.

During our time on the bus, I would read aloud excerpts of my father's writings before we arrived at a certain place. For me the most difficult place to visit was the camp of Majdanek. My father had endured Majdanek for five months. Majdanek appears **Majdanek** as if nothing has happened since the war. Of the Majdanek Torture Camp, my father writes, "One usually mentions Majdanek in one breath with Treblinka but there is a significant difference. Treblinka was a death camp only. The people lasted merely a few hours there, but Majdanek, which destroyed so many people, tortured its victims for weeks and months before killing them. There the soul was deadened first, then the body destroyed. Human beings lost every vestige of humanity. The cruelest sadists used the most refined and sophisticated tortures."

People tried to do a bit of business using their very few possessions, but to no avail; all that they buried was found and dug up by the Nazis. Upon arriving at the Majdanek camp, my father told me, newcomers were stopped before entering the camp, and commanded to strip before going to the showers. The path leading to the showers included numerous cruel tortures by the Czech doctors who checked every part of the body. The disinfection process itself was torturous. During this trek to the showers all their personal property disappeared, and the prisoners exited from the showers with used clothing that did not fit, a yellow star of David and an identification number. The concentration camp is huge, very cold, open (my father had arrived at the camp during the same season of the year that we were now standing at the camp). Since much of the camp remained as it had once been, I could easily identify the wooden disinfection bath, which my father had written about, and the showers. In Majdanek there are storage rooms containing thousands of pairs of shoes. This is the most tangible thing there today. In addition there are many exhibitions. I decided to wander among the prisoner blocks, to see how they looked inside. My father had been in Area 3 Block 22. When I entered the block area, I found that, quite by coincidence, I had entered Area 3 (there were 5 areas), Block 19.

Block 19, according to my father's story, was the clinic. The clinic was the last stop — no one ever returned from there; its only exit was the crematorium. And in spite of this, people still desired to get to the clinic. Behind the huge open areas, wrote my father the same large areas of grass that were used for inspections where people were forced to stand for hours, the chimneys of the crematoria could be seen. Everyone knew what was there. The open areas are long, and in fact separate the various sections of the camp. From the open area, one can see the city of Lublin, nothing obstructs the city from view, as nothing hides view to the camp. I stood on the freezing open lawn, with the bone-chilling wind penetrating my sweater and coat, and gazed at Lublin. The residents of the city knew exactly what was going on but did nothing. I wanted to shout to them, "Where, in God's name were you?" At the end of all the huts one arrives at the rows of crematoria where the ashes of the Jews who were killed there still remain. There we once again said Kaddish.

When we returned again to Warsaw, it was Friday, and we went to the synagogue for evening prayers. We arrived early and there was time to sit together as a group. We all sat there, silent, each one of us absorbed in his own thoughts. In these minutes I recalled aloud that in Jewish tradition even when one is mourning the death of a mother or father, one rises from mourning on Shabbat. Thus we all did rise together, and this experience helped all us free ourselves from all that we had been through in Auschwitz and Majdanek. Shabbat helped us break free of the difficult atmosphere pervading our journey until this point.

Israel 2003

I would like to add at this point that my two daughters, Shuli and Esti, both visited Poland and the Concentration Camps on school trips. Esti is serving in the Israeli Army at the present time. Unfortunately, these organized trips to Poland were not so acceptable when my eldest son, Yoel, who is currently completing an MBA in Melbourne Australia, was in high school in Israel. These trips to Poland are an important part of the education of each Jewish teenager, and I feel it was vitally significant for my children to see the places where their grandfather suffered and survived — and the rest of the family perished. Shuli wrote many poems after seeing the Camps in 1994. One poem is presented on the inside jacket of this book. She is currently studying for a B.A. in Communal Theater at Tel Aviv University.

In Summary: For the Sake of Jewish Peoplehood

My current professional work is dedicated to research and facilitation of what I call Jewish Peoplehood. In this pursuit I have served as Co-Founder and Chairman of Project Oren. Project Oren is today an integral part of Oranim Academic College of Education. Oranim, besides being Israel's largest institution of teacher training, is the base for many programs in Jewish identity, informal education and community building. Within Shdemot, the Center for Community Leadership at Oranim, Oren's mission is to promote Jewish Peoplehood by working with Jewish communities around the world. In fifteen years of activity, Oren has designed and implemented educational programs to address the needs of a spectrum of clientele from Israel and the Diaspora including: students, young adults, families, educators, and community leaders. Oren's mission of bringing Diaspora students to Israel for a kibbutz Israel Experience, as well as bringing families, Jewish educators and lay leaders, constitutes the "bare bones" of the vision of Jewish People-building.

JPB (as we affectionately call it) is a grand vision: it calls for Israel to become a central part of the lives of Diaspora Jews and Diaspora Judaism, while at the same time, Diaspora Jews and Diaspora communities will become part of the everyday consciousness of Israeli Jews. Finally, at the close of 2003, Oranim has established the new Center for the Study of the Jewish People, which I now head. This center includes senior educators working primarily in Israel as well as those working primarily with the Diaspora. Together these educators are building a common educational vision and program.

My professional work is part of my identity as a Jew and as the son of my parents. Israel by itself or a Diaspora community by itself is only a partial expression of Jewish Peoplehood. The vitality and viability of the Jewish people can be maintained only by the ongoing relationship between Israel and the Diaspora. It is a mistake to rely only on rabbis, performers or other charismatic figures. Most institutions of contemporary Jewish life are narrowly limited to certain selected interests. Culture is the fabric that binds the Jewish people together.

The Partnership 2000 project of the Jewish Agency is one practical way to actualize these goals of binding Israel with Diaspora communities. I have been involved in this project from its inception. Schools in Israel are matched up with Jewish schools abroad; teachers are matched with teachers and communities with communities — for example, Haifa is matched with Boston and

Yokneam-Megiddo is matched with Atlanta and St. Louis in the United States. The networks of these partnerships are multi-tiered, based on the reciprocity of person-to-person relationships.

My professional and personal life is inextricably intertwined. Major insights I have learned can be summarized in some essential lessons. First, are:

Lessons

Lessons from the life of my Father

- Lack of morality can never be excused by the circumstances.
- Historical memory is our guardian; personal responsibility is our obligation.
- Hope and optimism are our closest allies and constant companions.
- Not reception of the Torah but its affirmation is the key.

Lessons from my own life

- The Jewishness of Israel is not given, nor static, nor to be taken for granted; it must be guaranteed anew by each generation, in its turn, in its own time, in its own image.
- Similarly, Jewish Peoplehood, which is the primordial raison d'etre of the Jewish State, cannot be taken for granted. Each global Jewish generation must visit Sinai by itself, thereby taking part in an existential experience transcending time and place.

Wherein lies the point of the story?

My life has been experienced through multiple identities within a bridging frame of reference of Jewish Peoplehood. In Australia, these multiple identities included the Religious/Secular, Zionist/Non Zionist, Left/Right, Jewish Community/General Society and finally Israel/Diaspora. All these led me in Australia to see the following:

- Aliya as a commandment

• Israel experience as an educational strategy
• Jewish Peoplehood as my existential framework

In Israel, I encountered a prevalence of rejection and negation. My Zionist movement rejected the past, the religious and the Diaspora. The Left and the Labor regime I supported rejected the religious, the Right, Old and New Immigrants and the Holocaust survivors. Eventually the regime was repaid in kind, with interest, by being dumped by the people. Israel's democracy has valiantly struggled, yet failed to include its Arab citizens within a shared vision of the State and its future.

What is to be done?

• Build bridges between the Jewish community in Israel and the Jewish community in the Diaspora that are free of reciprocal rejection.
• Build each other's Jewish identity rather than building on the rejection of the identity of the other.
• Build each other's Jewish community in order to enhance each other's Jewish and general social capital. Utilize personal interconnectedness and community institutional interpenetration to determine each other's fate. Put bluntly, to build anew a vital Jewish people for our time.
• Build a State whose mission of sustaining Global Jewish Peoplehood can never be at the expense of the human rights, welfare and social justice of any of its citizens.

Much has been said about the future of Jewish communities in the Diaspora, but what of the Jewish community in Israel, particularly my Jewish community in Israel? My choice to live on a kibbutz was based both on its being an alternative community from the perspective of universal and socialist values as well as being a community with a Jewish vision. Today it is commonplace in Israel to claim that the kibbutz is an anachronism, an entity that has passed its peak, bereft both of its values as well as its means for independent collective physical survival. Sadly, for a growing number of kibbutzim some of these observations apply; happily, however, this is not the case for my home, Kibbutz Yizreel. Kibbutz Yizreel has consistently and intentionally recruited members from heterogeneous social sources both from within Israel and from the Diaspora for over four decades and has learned with a collective intuition the meaning of social capital and the art of its generation and maintenance. Thus, Kibbutz Yizreel, a relatively young and medium sized kibbutz, still maintains its collective ethos and egalitarian lifestyle more or less unscathed. What has become of its Jewish vision?

Community

Recently, an event occurred in my kibbutz that gives me personal hope for the future of Jewish Peoplehood. As a teenager and university student, I had rejected the strict practice of Judaism as archaic and irrelevant to my life as a student radical, Labor Zionist youth politician, and professional person. In Australia I shared with my family the cycle of the Jewish year in Shabbat and holidays. After making Aliya, I continued to keep a certain amount of traditional Jewish observance. But I have always lived with contradictions. I am neither religious nor secular and have managed to balance these tendencies in my own life. In general, Israelis have always been polarized in religion or politics. I used to come up against more anti-religious prejudices from secular Israelis than

I ever did from non-Jews in Australia. But things are changing in Israel. There are signs of growing tolerance and rapprochement between the extremes.

My completely "secular" kibbutz has always held Rosh Hashana and Yom Kippur services as well as Bar Mitzvah services (for most of the boys) in an empty classroom. Recently, the Ministry of Religion of the Israeli Government offered to donate a building for a synagogue with no strings attached. However, some kibbutz members feared this would be an opening for unwelcome religious coercion in the future. So, instead of a routine notice in the kibbutz newspaper, we held a large general meeting, where the issue was vociferously debated — and the vote was to accept the Synagogue. I now help lead weekly Shabbat services in our new synagogue for about fifteen to twenty participants, almost all of whom are kibbutz members in their thirties and forties. Even non-participants have approached me, saying, "I was against it at first; now I'm pleased we have a synagogue."

I hope this points to the beginning of greater tolerance and understanding in Kibbutz Yizreel — in Israel and Klal Yisrael.

Epilogue

During my trip to Poland I let my traveling companions share my grandfather's story. After we saw his house in Warsaw I read out a section of the testimony he wrote and afterwards I sat in my place and wrote.

I walk in the streets of Poland and try to imagine you walking in the streets. How did you manage? Did you see all the green that I saw? I feel closer to you now than ever, brave man — loving and strong. It's sad for me that you never would know my existence at all and I, on the other hand, did not merit meeting your special presence. How can a human being confront the atrocities you saw in your life? From where did you draw the physical and spiritual strength to see bodies around you, terrible hunger and the painful parting from your family? Grandfather, you are my hero — you who never lost hope in life, who was victorious over the Nazi oppressor and who showed the world that Judaism would never be buried in the soil of Poland. I listen to my heart and it longs to meet you, to ask you questions even without receiving answers.

Now on the seventh day of my trip to Poland, everything is coming out of me; perhaps I have finally understood — certainly not completely. I want to thank you for opening old wounds so that I may read and learn the stories in the hope that I will not have to deal with wounds like these. Grandfather, you are the stable root that has been plucked up from its place, stubbornly returning to give life to its flowers. To your credit our family is flowering in a range of colors not forgetting the earth from which it is nourished. Grandfather, even though I never met you, I feel longing for the man who succeeded in ascending from the depths of the abyss to beyond the expanse of freedom.

Grandfather, thank you for not losing hope and for causing me to follow your footsteps. I believe that I now understand the meaning of a united supportive family, the basic morality of man where ever he may be, and, essentially, the powerful will to live — the feeling that I will not break down before the obstacles placed before me and that I will guard my true self and I will not allow others to trample tradition and the Jewish people.

Grandfather, wait for me where you are — and one day we will meet.

Rest in peace,
Your loving grand-daughter, Esti
Warsaw 2001